Fantastic
Fairies
and their friends

Fantastic
Fairies
and their friends

Julie Sharp

GUILD OF
MASTER CRAFTSMAN
PUBLICATIONS

A lovely team of people aren't they!

First published 2006 by **Guild of Master Craftsman Publications Ltd**. Castle Place, 166 High Street, Lewes, East Sussex BN7 1XU

Text and illustrations © Julie Sharp 2006
© in the Work GMC Publications 2006
Photographs by Anthony Bailey

ISBN 1 86108 462 5

Production Manager: Hilary MacCallum
Managing Editor: Gerrie Purcell
Project Editor: Dominique Page
Managing Art Editor: Gilda Pacitti
Designer: Rebecca Mothersole

Set in AvantGarde and TypoUpright
Colour origination by Altaimage
Printed and bound by Kyodo, Singapore

A Note About The Measurements
Conversions are approximate. Use either metric or imperial; do not mix measurements.

In Memory Of
Ivor Hampton Sharp 1928–1989
Painter, photographer,
Inspiring teacher,
Father, "love you all the universe".

A few words from the author

I developed the wrapping technique used in this book out of an involvement with art demonstrations at school fêtes. The projects join together wrapped pompoms and pipe-cleaners, building layers of material that can be stitched and shaped into designs that are robust enough to be played with. Characters made from straightforward material provide a stimulating activity for children of all ages. The techniques are forgiving and versatile and become easier the more you practise.

The most challenging aspect of the fairy projects is shaping facial features. A decent flesh-coloured yarn in either 2- or 4-ply gauge will influence the outcome of your technique. Try shades and textures to see what works best and experiment with nose and chin sizes, hairlines and hair lengths. Keep practising; your technique improves with every attempt.

The Fairy Moth, Buggle Fairy and Florabea Fairy projects are the easiest to make. Bud the Mouse and Fairy Butterfly are the most simple wrap pompom projects. The Tree Hideaway, Toadstool and Pumpkin Hideaway have the greatest number of pompoms and will take up more time than other projects. Get family and friends to wrap with you.

Visit my website at:
www.createchures.com

We're great fun to play with!

Contents

Meet the Characters

Fairy Clothes & Accessories

Fairy Homes & Hideaways

Creating your Fairy World

Meet the Characters

The Fairy Empress is the most basic character to make using the wrapping technique. She is soft, flexible, and easily dressed in costumes.

Fairy Empress

What you need:

Materials

* 2oz (50g) ball of white fashion yarn
* 2oz (50g) ball of white-flecked yarn
* 2oz (50g) ball of peach yarn
* 1/8in (3mm) white ready-made pompoms x 2
* 12 x 3/16in (300 x 5mm) pale pink pipe-cleaners x 6
* 12 x 3/16in (300 x 5mm) yellow striped pipe-cleaner

* White thread
* 4 x 4in (100 x 100mm) plastic sheet
* Green permanent marker pen

Tools

* Embroidery scissors
* Craft scissors
* Small cardboard platform **(see page 118)**
* Craft needle
* Sewing needle

Head

⭐ **1** Wrap the peach yarn around the small cardboard platform 70 times then do the same with the white fashion yarn to create a two-colour pompom **(see page 130)**.

⭐ **2** Trim the white part to make a head shape then use embroidery scissors to contour the peach part into an oval face. (A)

⭐ **3** Using the same scissors, carefully shape chubby cheeks, a nose, smiling mouth and hollows for eyes. Sew the two white ⅛in (3mm) ready-made pompoms into the hollows for eyeballs then use the green marker to draw pupils. Add a couple of stitches of peach yarn level with the eyes and overlapping the hairline to form ears. (B)

⭐ **4** Lengthen the white hairline by weaving more of the yarn through the forehead, top, back and sides. (C)

⭐ **5** Braid a 10in (250mm) length of white fashion yarn using three strands. Fold the braid in half and attach the centre to the back of the head to form two long hair braids. (D)

Antennae

⭐ **6** Make antennae with the yellow striped pipe-cleaner. Curl the ends then fold in half. Sew to the top of the head with the white fashion yarn. (E)

Neck

⭐ **7** Take a 1in (25mm) piece of pale pink pipe-cleaner and wrap the ends with the peach yarn. Fold the ends over then wrap the middle.

Body

⭐ **8** Combine some white fashion yarn and white-flecked yarn. Wrap the mixed yarn 60 times around the small cardboard platform to make a pompom **(see page 129)**. Make another in the same way. These will form the chest and bottom of the Fairy Empress. Sew the two pompoms together with white-flecked yarn. Trim the middle to create a waistline (copy the diagram). (F)

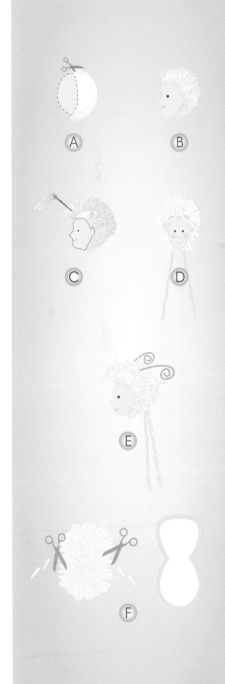

A

B

C

D

E

F

I roll along in my chariot when I'm not flying.

9 Weave additional white-flecked yarn into the upper chest and bottom to build them up. Trim to shape. G

Arms

10 Make a set of Type 2 arms **(see page 142)**. Wrap them with peach yarn. Weave white-flecked yarn around the shoulders to build them up and then trim to shape. H

Legs

11 Make a set of Type 2 legs **(see page 138)** and wrap them with peach yarn. I

Wings

12 Make a set of wings using the templates on **page 146.** J

Putting the Fairy Empress together

13 Place the base of the body onto the middle of the leg bar then sew them together with white-flecked yarn. K

14 Place the shoulder bar of the arms onto the top of the body and attach with white-flecked yarn. Wrap the shoulder bar with white fashion yarn to blend the shoulders in with the rest of the body. L

15 Sew the neck to the head and then sew both to centre of the shoulder bar. Pass the yarn through the core of the body to anchor the head. To complete the Fairy Empress sew on her wings with white fashion yarn, overlapping them with the larger pair on top and the smaller pair below. M

The Grass Sprite has a soft, flexible body with a curly tail and is similar in size to the Empress. He loves his bright boots and comfy pumpkin to hide in.

Grass Sprite

What you need:

Materials

* 2oz (50g) ball of yellow-green fashion yarn
* 2oz (50g) ball of peach yarn
* 2oz (50g) ball of pale green yarn
* $1/8$in (3mm) white ready-made pompoms x 2
* 12 x $3/16$in (300 x 5mm) pale pink pipe-cleaners x 6
* $5/16$ x $3/16$in (8 x 5mm) flecked orange pipe-cleaner
* 5 x 4in (125 x 100mm) plastic sheet
* Blue permanent marker pen
* Orange permanent marker pen
* Yellow permanent marker pen

Tools

* Embroidery scissors
* Craft scissors
* Small cardboard platform **(see page 118)**
* Craft/sewing needle

Head

1   Wrap the peach yarn 70 times around the small cardboard platform then do the same with the yellow-green fashion yarn to create a two-colour pompom **(see page 130).**

2   Trim the yellow-green half into a head shape and the peach half into a thin oval face shape. (A)

3   Using embroidery scissors, contour a nose, cheeks and hollows for eyes. Now sew the 1/8in (3mm) white ready-made pompoms into the hollows for eyeballs and use the blue marker to draw dots for pupils. Draw a faint smile with an orange marker and eyebrows with a yellow marker. Create ears by sewing two stitches of peach yarn, overlapping the yellow-green half. (B)

4   Now weave some yellow-green fashion yarn into the forehead, top back and sides to create a hairline. (C)

Antennae

5   Trim the flecked orange pipe-cleaner so that it is thin. Curl the ends then fold in half and attach the centre to the top of the head with the yellow-green fashion yarn. (D)

Neck

6   Take a 1in (25mm) piece of pale pink pipe-cleaner and wrap the ends with the peach yarn. Fold the ends over then wrap the middle.

Body

7   Wrap the yellow-green yarn 120 times around the small cardboard platform to make a pompom. Make another in the same way. These will form Grass Sprite's chest and bottom.

8   Sew together the chest and bottom pompoms using the yellow-green yarn. Trim the middle section into a man's straight waistline (copy the diagram). (E)

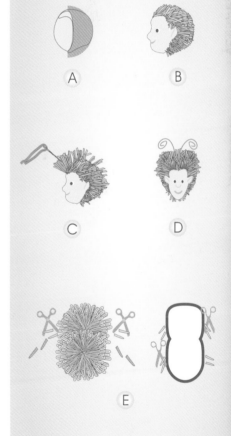

15

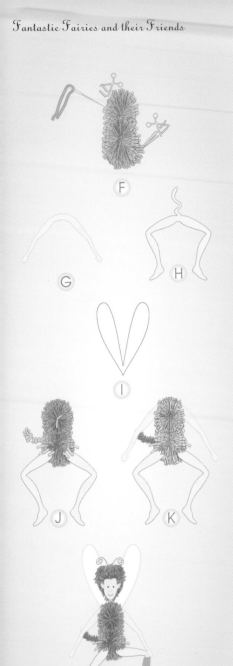

9 The back of Sprite should have a bulge and a loose, fluffy texture, so weave a few wispy threads into the bottom of this section. Weave some extra yellow-green yarn into the upper shoulder and chest area to build them up. Trim the yarn added to the shoulders. (F)

Arms

10 Make a set of Type 2 arms **(see page 142)** and wrap with the peach yarn. (G)

Legs

11 Make a set of Type 1 legs **(see page 135)** and wrap with the peach yarn. (Optional: Grass Sprite has a pair of boots **(see page 68)** and usually wears grass socks for warmth, so wrap green yarn above the ankle to below the knee for Grass Sprite socks.) (H)

Wings

12 Make a pair of wings from a plastic sheet using the template on **page 147**. (I)

Putting the Grass Sprite together

13 Place the bottom of the body onto the leg and tail bar. Sew in place with the yellow-green yarn. Wrap the tail with this yarn to blend in with the body. Curl and shape the the tail around your finger. (J)

14 Sew the arms into the shoulder area with yellow-green yarn. Cover the shoulders with more of this yarn but leave a space for the neck. (K)

15 Attach the neck to the head and then sew both to the centre of the shoulder bar. Weave yellow-green yarn through the core of the body to anchor them in place. Finally, attach the wings to the back, just below the shoulders. (L)

*The Ladybug Fairy has a sturdy round figure
and plenty of arms to grab things.*

Ladybug Fairy

What you need:

Materials

* 2oz (50g) ball of dark orange yarn
* 2oz (50g) ball of dark grey yarn
* 2oz (50g) ball of pale brown yarn
* $1/8$in (3mm) white ready-made pompoms x 2
* 12 x $3/16$in (300 x 5mm) brown pipe-cleaners x 6
* White thread
* Green permanent marker
* Orange permanent marker
* 4in x $1^1/2$in (100 x 35mm) plastic sheet

Tools

* Embroidery scissors
* Craft scissors
* Small cardboard platform **(see page 118)**
* Craft/sewing needle

Head

1. Wrap the brown yarn 70 times around the small cardboard platform then do the same with the grey yarn to create a two-colour pompom **(see page 130)**.

2. Trim the grey half into a head shape and the brown half into a thin oval face. (A)

3. Using embroidery scissors carefully contour the face to create round chubby cheeks, a nose and hollows for eyes. Sew ⅛in (3mm) white pompoms into the hollows for eyeballs then use the green permanent marker to draw dots for pupils. Draw a faint mouth with the orange marker pen. Sew a couple of pale brown yarn stitches overlapping the grey half to form ears. (B)

4. Sew a few stitches of grey yarn overlapping the forehead to create a hairline. Weave grey yarn over the head to make hair loops Position the loops onto the top, back, sides and forehead for a hairline. (C)

Neck

5. Make a neck using a 1in (25mm) piece of brown pipe-cleaner. Make loops at both ends then fold the loops over and wrap them with brown yarn. Now wrap the whole neck with four layers of grey yarn to make a thick neck.

Body

6. Wrap orange yarn 120 times around the small cardboard platform then do the same with the grey yarn to make a two-colour pompom. Trim the grey half with craft scissors to create an oval, domed stomach.

7. Make a rounded back from the orange area, only trimming lightly so that it is still nice and thick. (D)

8. Trim a canal down the centre to separate it into two sections then weave grey spots on both sides, weaving through the stomach. (E)

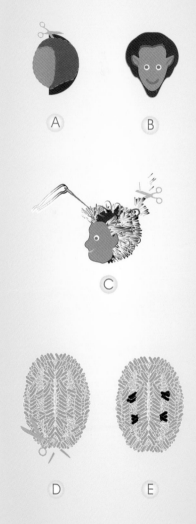

A

B

C

D

E

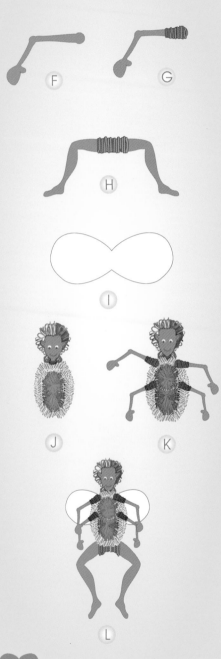

Arms

9 Make four arm pods using two brown pipe-cleaners **(see page 145)**. Cut the arms into two sections and loop the ends. Now make hands and thumbs **(see page 145)**. Wrap three layers of brown yarn around the arms and embroider elbow lumps onto the middle of both sets of arms. F

10 Wrap the looped ends with orange yarn, covering about ½in (12mm), to create short sleeves. G

Legs

11 Make a set of Type 2 legs **(see page 138)** then wrap with brown yarn. To make the Ladybug Fairy's knickers, cover 1in (25mm) at the centre of the leg frame with orange yarn. H

Wings

12 Now make a pair of wings from a plastic sheet using the template on **page 147**. I

Putting Ladybug together

13 Use orange yarn to sew the neck to the head and then both to the top of the body, ½in (12mm) away from the grey section. J

14 Use orange yarn to attach one pair of arms to the shoulder section of the orange body in front of the neck. Position the second set of arms ½in (12mm) underneath to the side of the grey stomach area. Attach with orange yarn through the back of the body. K

15 Attach the legs under the front of the body, just beneath the grey stomach area, by weaving orange yarn through the legs and knickers into the core of the orange body area. Finally, attach the wings to the back of Ladybug Fairy with orange yarn. Line them up with her top pair of arms, just below her shoulders. L

Sometimes when I eat too much my tummy feels as big as my prize-winning onion!

21

The Dragonfly Fairy has flaming colours and blends well with autumn leaves. She has a soft, flexible and sturdy body, similar to the Grass Sprite.

Dragonfly Fairy

What you need:

Materials

* 2oz (50g) ball of crimson-and-green-flecked fashion yarn
* 2oz (50g) ball of crimson yarn
* 2oz (50g) ball of golden beige yarn
* 1/8in (3mm) white ready-made pompoms x 2
* 12 x 3/16in (300 x 5mm) pale pink pipe-cleaners x 8
* Blue permanent marker pen

* 12 x 3/16in (300 x 5mm) yellow striped pipe-cleaner
* 11 x 4in (280 x 100mm) plastic sheet

Tools

* Embroidery scissors
* Craft scissors
* Small cardboard platform **(see page 118)**
* Craft needle

I feel more colourful when I'm with my friends!

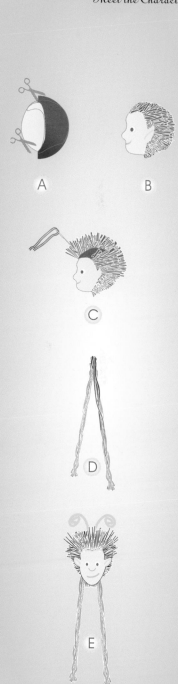

B

C

D

E

Head

1. Wrap the beige yarn 70 times around the small cardboard platform then do the same with the crimson fashion yarn to create a two-colour pompom **(see page 130)**.

2. Trim the crimson half into a head shape and the beige half into a thin oval face. (A)

3. Using embriodery scissors, carefully contour cheeks, a nose and hollows for eyes. Sew the ⅛in (3mm) white ready-made pompoms into the hollows for eyeballs then use a blue permanent marker pen to draw dots for pupils. Add a couple of stitches of beige yarn level with the eyes and overlapping the hairline to create ears. (B)

4. Place a few stitches of the crimson fashion yarn slightly overlapping the forehead to create a hairline. Weave some more of this yarn through the top, back, sides and forehead. (C)

5. Braid a 15in (380mm) length of crimson fashion yarn using six strands. Fold in half then attach the centre to the back of the head, but slightly off to one side. (D)

Antennae

6. Trim the pile of the yellow striped pipe-cleaner to make it thinner then curl the ends. Fold in half and attach the centre to the back of the head with crimson fashion yarn. (E)

Neck

7. Take a 1in (25mm) piece of pale pink pipe-cleaner and wrap the ends with the beige yarn. Fold the ends over then wrap the middle. Use one of the folds to thread peach yarn through and sew to the head.

Body and tail

8. Wrap the crimson fashion yarn 120 times around the small cardboard platform to make a pompom **(see page 129)**. Create five more in the same way to form the chest, bottom and tail pompoms.

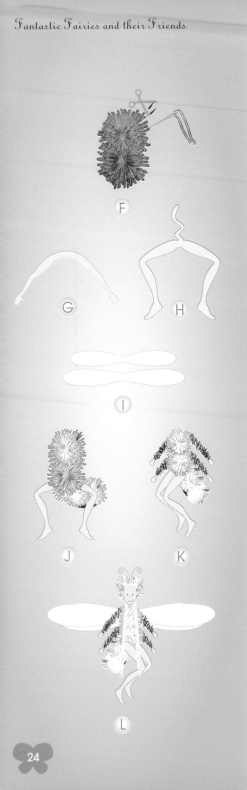

9 Take the two body pompoms and sew together using the crimson yarn. Lightly trim the shoulder area to round it out.

10 Weave crimson fashion yarn into the upper shoulder and chest area to build them up a bit then trim this additional yarn to shape. The bottom area, however, should have a loose, fluffy texture. (F)

Arms

11 Make two sets of Type 2 arms **(see page 142)** then wrap with the beige yarn. (G)

Legs

12 Make a set of Type 1 legs **(see page 135)** then wrap with the beige yarn. (H)

Wings

13 Now make a set of wings from a plastic sheet using the templates on **page 146**. (I)

Putting Dragonfly Fairy together

14 Sew the bottom of the body onto the leg and tail bar with the crimson fashion yarn. Now wrap the tail with the crimson fashion yarn then sew the tail pompoms underneath the tail frame and the bottom pompom. (J)

15 Sew one set of arms to the shoulder area. Once in place, wrap the arms down to the wrists with crimson fashion yarn to create long sleeves. Sew the other set of arms to the middle of the body and give this set of arms sleeves, too. (K)

16 Sew the neck and head to the centre of the shoulders. Now weave crimson fashion yarn through the core of the body to secure them. Finally, overlap the wing pieces and sew them to the back shoulders with crimson fashion yarn. (L)

Florabea is a fledgling fairy without antennae. She has a head that turns, tiny wings, and legs and arms that bend and hold things.

Florabea Fairy

What you need:

Materials

* 3in (75mm) beige pipe-cleaner
* 1½in (35mm) beige pipe-cleaners x 2
* ⅜in (10mm) glittery pink ready-made pompom
* ⅜in (10mm) beige ready-made pompom
* ⅛in (3mm) beige ready-made pompoms x 2
* ⅜in (10mm) glittery green ready-made pompoms x 2
* ⅛in (3mm) green ready-made pompoms x 2
* 1in (25mm) plastic sheets x 2
* White thread
* Green permanent marker pen
* Pink permanent marker pen

Tools

* Sewing needle
* Craft scissors

Head

⭐ 1 Snip a flat area from the back of a ⅜in (10mm) beige 'face' pompom and sew on a glittery pink pompom to the back to make hair. (A)

⭐ 2 Sew a ⅛in (3mm) beige pompom to the centre of the face to make a nose. Now use a green permanent marker pen to add two eye dots above the nose and a pink permanent marker to give Florabea a smiling mouth. (B)

Body

⭐ 3 Sew together two ⅜in (10mm) glittery green pompoms. (C)

Legs

⭐ 4 Bend a 3in (75mm) beige pipe-cleaner in half. Fold over the ends by ½in (12mm) to make each foot. Clip away little sections of the pile to make ankles. (D)

Arms

⭐ 5 Take two 1½in (35mm) beige pipe-cleaners. Fold the ends of each to make small loops. Fold these over by ¼in (5mm) to make hands. Now clip little sections of the pile to create tiny wrists. (E)

Wings

⭐ 6 Cut a set of wings using the templates on **page 147**. (F)

Putting Florabea together

⭐ 7 Sew a ⅛in (3mm) beige 'neck' pompom to the head then sew the neck and head to the body, passing thread through the core of the body to secure. (G)

⭐ 8 Connect the legs to the body by sewing the top bend of the leg into the bottom pompom. Now sew the ⅛in (3mm) green pompoms at the sides of the chest for shoulders and the arm loops onto the shoulders. (H)

⭐ 9 Finally, sew on the smallest section of wing to Florabea's back. Overlap with the larger piece, positioning it just above the first. (I)

The Fairy Moth is quick and easy to assemble in any colour using ready-made pompoms and pipe-cleaners.

Fairy Moth

What you need:

Materials

* ✳ 3in (75mm) peach pipe-cleaner
* ✳ 1½in (35mm) peach pipe-cleaner x 2
* ✳ 4½in (115mm) pink pipe-cleaner
* ✳ ⅜in (10mm) pink ready-made pompoms x 3
* ✳ ⅛in (3mm) pink ready-made pompoms x 2
* ✳ Pink crayon

* ✳ ³⁄₁₆in (5mm) pink ready-made pompoms x 2
* ✳ 3¼ x 2¼in (80 x 55mm) plastic sheet
* ✳ White thread
* ✳ Orange or brown permanent marker pen

Tools

* ✳ Sewing needle
* ✳ Craft scissors

Head

1   Sew a ⅛in (3mm) pink pompom to the centre of a ⅜in (10mm) pink pompom to create a face and nose. Use a marker pen to add two eye dots above the nose. (A)

Antennae

2   Trim the pink pipe-cleaner so that it is thin. Curl the ends and bend in half. Sew to the top of the head. (B)

Neck

3   Sew a ⅛in (3mm) pink pompom to the head to create a neck.

Body

4   Sew two pink ⅜in (10mm) pompoms together with thread. (C)

Arms

5   Take the two 1½in (35mm) peach pipe-cleaners. Fold the ends of each to make small loops. Fold these over by ¼in (5mm) to make hands. Now clip little sections of the pile to create Fairy Moth's wrists. (D)

Legs

6   Bend the 3in (75mm) peach pipe-cleaner in half. Fold over the ends by ½in (12mm) to make each foot. Clip away little sections of the pile to make ankles. (E)

Wings

7   Cut a small pair of wings using the template on **page 147**. Colour the wings with pink crayon. (F)

Putting Fairy Moth together

8   Attach the head and neck to the body by sewing thread through the core of the body to secure. (G)

9   Sew the arms at either side of the chest and legs to the centre of the bottom pompom. (H)

10   To finish, sew two tail pompoms underneath the legs and attach the wings to the back of the chest with white thread. (I)

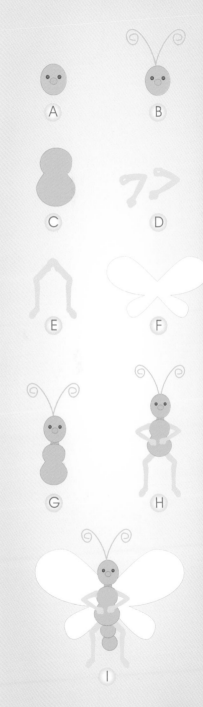

29

Buggles are bright fairy creatures that buzz about with little wings.
Ready-made pompoms are the main components, plus a trimmed pipe-cleaner.

Buggle Fairy

What you need:

Materials

* ⅛in (3mm) grey ready-made pompoms x 2
* ³⁄₁₆in (5mm) orange ready-made pompoms x 3
* ⅛in (3mm) orange ready-made pompoms x 20
* ⅛in (3mm) white ready-made pompoms x 2
* ⅜in (10mm) orange ready-made pompoms x 2
* Orange crayon
* ⅝in (15mm) orange ready-made pompoms x 2
* ¾in (20mm) orange ready-made pompom
* 6in (150mm) orange pipe-cleaner
* Orange thread
* White thread
* 1in (25mm) plastic sheets x 2
* Green permanent marker pen

Tools

* Sewing needle
* Embroidery scissors

Head

⭐ Take the ¾in (20mm) orange pompom and attach a ³⁄₁₆in (5mm) orange pompom to the centre to form a face and nose. Using embroidery scissors, clip away a small amount from the top of the larger pompom to shape the Buggle's head. (A)

⭐ Sew two ⅛in (3mm) orange pompoms to the forehead to create eyelids and position two ⅛in (3mm) white pompoms underneath for eyeballs. Use a green permanent marker to add pupils. To create a smile, use embroidery scissors to carefully remove a curved line of pile from below the nose. (B)

Antennae

⭐ Trim the 6in (150mm) orange pipe-cleaner so that it is thin then curl the ends and bend in half. Attach the antennae to the back of the head. (C)

Neck

⭐ Sew two ³⁄₁₆in (5mm) orange pompoms together. (D)

Body

⭐ Take a ⅝in (15mm) pompom and trim a tiny amount from one area to make a flat contact point. Sew this to another ⅝in (15mm) pompom. (E)

Legs and Arms

⭐ Sew four ⅛in (3mm) pompoms together with orange thread. Make up four columns for the legs and arms. (F)

⭐ Sew two ⅜in (10mm) orange pompoms onto two of the columns for feet. Snip the bottom of the feet to flatten them. (G)

⭐ Sew two ⅛in (3mm) orange pompoms onto the other two columns for hands. (H)

Wings

⭐ Cut a small pair of wings using the template on **page 147**. Colour with an orange crayon. (I)

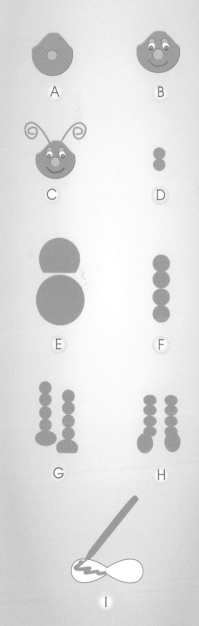

A B C D E F G H I

31

J   K

L

M

Putting Buggle together

⭐ 10 Sew the legs to the bottom pompom, spacing them ³⁄₈in (10mm) apart. Ⓙ

⭐ 11 Attach the arms to the chest at shoulder level. Ⓚ

⭐ 12 Sew the neck to the top of the chest then attach the head to the neck, sewing through the chest to secure. Pull the thread taught to compress the chest shape. Ⓛ

⭐ 13 Finally, sew two ¹⁄₈in (3mm) grey pompoms onto Buggle's waistline for a stylish belt and sew the wings onto Buggle's back. Ⓜ

I love to have my back rubbed.

This fairy character has a soft, floppy body that bends into engaging poses. His large wing span is decorated with pencils and is fun to colour.

Butterfly Fairy

What you need:

Materials

* 2oz (50g) ball of dark grey yarn
* 2oz (50g) ball of black fashion yarn
* ¹⁄₈in (3mm) white ready-made pompoms x 2
* ³⁄₈in (10mm) orange ready-made pompom
* ¹⁄₈in (3mm) bright pink ready-made pompoms x 7
* 9 x ³⁄₁₆in (230 x 5mm) black pipe-cleaners x 4

* Orange thread
* White thread

Tools

* Craft and embroidery scissors
* Sewing needle
* Knitting needle or chopstick for shaping hand pods
* Pencil for shaping foot pods
* Small cardboard platform **(see page 118)**

I dream of becoming the Fairy King.

Head

1 Wrap the black fashion yarn 100 times around the small cardboard platform to make a pompom **(see page 129)**.

2 Use white thread to sew the two white ¹⁄₈in (3mm) ready-made pompoms to the face for eyes. Sew the ³⁄₈in (10mm) orange 'nose' pompom just under the eyes. Ⓐ

Antennae

3 Make antennae with a black pipe-cleaner by bending it in half and curling the ends. Sew to the top of the head with black yarn. Ⓑ

Neck

4 Take a 1in (25mm) piece of black pipe-cleaner and wrap the ends with grey yarn. Fold the ends over then wrap the middle. Use one of the folds to thread grey yarn through and sew to the head.

Body and tail

5 Wrap the black fashion yarn 60 times around the small cardboard

platform then wrap the grey yarn 50 times next to it to make a two-colour pompom for Butterfly Fairy's bottom **(see page 130)**.

6 Make another black and grey pompom for Butterfly Fairy's chest by wrapping the black fashion yarn 60 times and the grey yarn also 60 times onto the small cardboard platform.

7 Trim the grey sections of both pompoms into circular shapes. Leave the black sides nice and hairy.

8 Wrap the grey yarn 60 times around the small cardboard platform to make a tail pompom.

9 Now sew the chest, bottom and tail pompoms together. Ⓒ

Arms

10 Next make arm pods with hands and thumbs **(see page 145)** from the remains of the black pipe-cleaner that you cut for the neck. Cover the arm pods with two layers of grey yarn

Ⓐ

Ⓑ

Ⓒ

D

E

F

G

H

I

and then wrap one layer of the black fashion yarn around just the arms. D

11 Now make arm pods with hand loops **(see page 145)** from a black pipe-cleaner and wrap with black fashion yarn. E

Legs

12 Using another black pipe-cleaner, create legs with foot pods **(see page 138).** Cover the feet and legs with the grey yarn. Wrap one layer of the black fashion yarn over both the feet and ankles to give Butterfly his hairy boots. F

Wings

13 Make a pair of wings using the template on **page 147**. Colour with purple and orange crayons. G

Putting Butterfly together

14 Attach the neck and head to the top of the chest using grey yarn. Sew through all the body pompoms.

15 Sew both sets of arms to the body with grey yarn. Position the first set of arm pods at the back of the neck and the second set between the chest and bottom pompoms at the back so that they wrap around to the front. Now use grey yarn to sew the legs between the tail and Butterfly's bottom. H

16 Weave additional yarn into any bare patches and trim stray grey threads so that the grey parts of the pompoms are neat and round.

17 Finally, sew Butterfly Fairy's wings to his back with orange thread and then for the finishing touch sew six pink ready-made pompoms down his spine. I

The Scatterpillar has a soft, curvy design and his 12 pod legs can be manipulated into wonderful curly poses.

Scatterpillar

What you need:

Materials

* 2oz (50g) ball of light green yarn
* 2oz (50g) ball of turquoise blue fashion yarn
* ³⁄₁₆in (5mm) black ready-made pompoms x 2
* ³⁄₈in (10mm) glittery green ready-made pompoms x 2
* 12 x ³⁄₁₆in (300 x 5mm) green or blue pipe-cleaners x 7
* White thread

* 6 x ³⁄₁₆in (150 x 5mm) green striped pipe-cleaner

Tools

* Sewing needle
* Craft needle
* Craft scissors
* Small cardboard platform **(see page 118)**
* Pencil for shaping foot pods

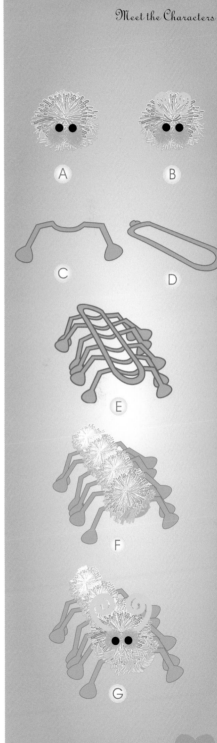

A

B

C

D

E

F

G

Head

1 Wrap the green yarn 80 times around the small cardboard platform then wrap the blue yarn 100 times next to it to create a two-colour pompom **(see page 130)**. Trim away any stray yarn from the green section to round the bottom of the face.

2 Sew the two ³⁄₈in (10mm) glittery green pompoms just below the blue fluffy yarn line then sew the ³⁄₁₆in (5mm) black pompoms to them to create Scatterpillar's eyes. A

Antennae

3 Make antennae with half a green striped pipe-cleaner. Curl the ends and bend in half. Attach the antennae to the front of the face above the blue fluffy yarn line. B

Body

4 Wrap the green yarn 70 times around the small cardboard platform then wrap the blue yarn 70 times next to it to create a two-colour pompom. Create four more in this way.

Legs

5 Make 12 leg pods **(see page 138)** using one pipe-cleaner for each pair of legs. Bend each leg frame slightly in the middle. Wrap the pod legs with the green yarn. C

6 Curve a pipe-cleaner then connect the ends. Pull at the sides to straighten into a long tubular frame. Wrap with green yarn. D

7 Place the leg pods across the frame, spacing them evenly, then sew them to the frame with green yarn. E

Putting Scatterpillar together

8 Sew the four body pompoms onto the frame, placing the green side down against the frame. F

9 Attach the head to the front of the body, sewing the green parts together. Finally, weave blue fashion yarn between the blue sections to fill in any patchy areas. G

Bud has tiny fabric ears, a small wrapped tail, legs and arms, plus a cute pompom nose and eyes. He is one of the easiest characters to make.

Bud the Mouse

What you need:

Materials

* ✴ 2oz (50g) ball of flecked white fashion yarn
* ✴ 2oz (50g) ball of peach yarn
* ✴ ⅛in (3mm) black ready-made pompoms x 2
* ✴ ⅛in (3mm) peach ready-made pompom
* ✴ 3 x 1½in (75 x 35mm) peach felt
* ✴ 12 x 3/16in (300 x 5mm) pink pipe-cleaners x 3

* ✴ White thread

Tools

* ✴ Craft scissors
* ✴ Yarn needle
* ✴ Sewing needle
* ✴ Small cardboard platform **(see page 118)**
* ✴ Medium cardboard platform **(see page 118)**

40

Head

⭐ Wrap the white fashion yarn 80 times around the small cardboard platform to make a pompom **(see page 129)**.

⭐ Using craft scissors, trim the pompom into a head shape. Ⓐ

⭐ Cut two ears from peach felt. Pinch the square lower part of one ear and sew together. Do the same with the other ear. Ⓑ

⭐ Sew the peach pompom nose, black pompom eyes and the ears onto the head with white thread. Ⓒ

Body

⭐ Wrap the white fashion yarn 120 times around the medium cardboard platform to make a pompom for Bud's bottom.

⭐ Wrap the white fashion yarn 100 times around the small cardboard platform to make a pompom for Bud's chest.

⭐ Trim both pompoms to shape but keep a wispy appearance.

⭐ Sew together the chest and bottom pompoms, with the chest set slightly back. Ⓓ

Arms and feet

⭐ Cut two pipe-cleaners in half and then fold the four pieces in half, looping the sharp ends together. Now wrap each piece with white fashion yarn, leaving the ends bare. Clip the pile from one end of each piece to create pointed claws. Ⓔ

Tail

⭐ Take a pipe-cleaner and fold it in half. Loop both the ends and then wrap it with three layers of peach yarn. Ⓕ

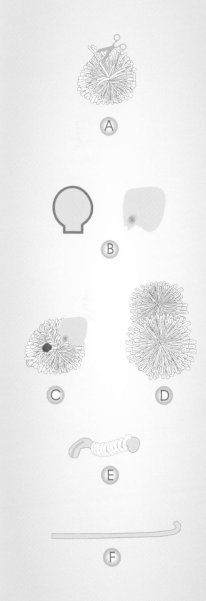

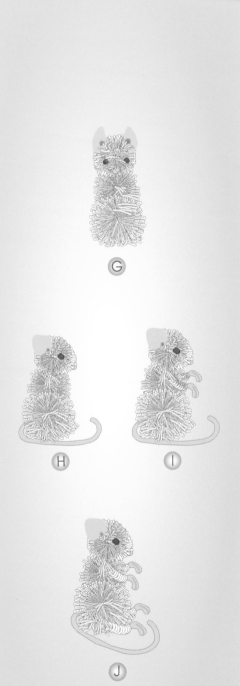

G

H

I

J

Piggy-backs are a great way to see the world.

13 Position the arms on either side of the chest at shoulder level. Weave white thread through the arms and chest pompom to secure. I

14 Position the legs underneath the body by placing the back leg loops near to the tail. Attach with white fashion yarn, weaving through the back leg loops and the bottom pompom. J

Putting Bud together

11 Place the head on top of the chest, setting it slightly forwards. Run white yarn through the three body pieces to secure them. G

12 Sew the tail to the bottom of Bud with white yarn and give it a slight curve. H

15 Finally, weave yarn into any bare patches and trim uneven threads to balance shape on all sides. Bud is now complete!

Sunny on top,
shady underneath.
A perfect place for
sunbathing.

The Baby Rabbit is very easy to make. She is similar to Bud the Mouse and Squirrel and, of course, just as attractive.

Baby Rabbit

What you need:

Materials
* 2oz (50g) ball of brown fashion yarn
* 2oz (50g) ball of white fashion yarn
* $3/16$in (5mm) black ready-made pompoms x 2
* $3/16$in (5mm) brown ready-made pompom
* 12 x $3/16$in (300 x 5mm) beige pipe-cleaners x 2

* Black thread
* Brown thread

Tools
* Craft scissors
* Yarn needle
* Sewing needle
* Small cardboard platform **(see page 118)**
* Medium cardboard platform **(see page 118)**

Head

☆1   Wrap brown fashion yarn 150 times around the small cardboard platform to create a pompom **(see page 129)**.

☆2   Shape the head and create a face by trimming into an oval. (A)

☆3   Sew on the black ready-made pompoms for eyes and the brown ready-made pompom for a nose. (B)

Ears

☆4   Take a 5in (125mm) piece of beige pipe-cleaner. Make a loop at one end. Use 3in (75mm) at the other end to form a circle, looping at the end to secure the circle. Make a point at the top and bottom to form a diamond shape and then pull the sides out slightly. (C)

☆5   Take the remaining 2in (50mm) of the pipe-cleaner and curve it upwards through the centre of the ear, bending the looped end onto the tip of the ear. (D)

☆6   Wrap the ear on both sides with the brown fashion yarn, weaving through the pipe-cleaner to secure it. Cover the back of the ear completely but leave the front open to form the cavity of the ear. (E)

☆7   Create a second ear in the same way and sew both to the rabbit's head, leaving about ¼in (5mm) between them. (F)

Body

☆8   Wrap the brown fashion yarn 120 times around the medium cardboard platform to create a pompom for Baby Rabbit's chest.

☆9   Now wrap the brown fashion yarn 200 times around the medium cardboard platform to create a pompom for Baby Rabbit's bottom.

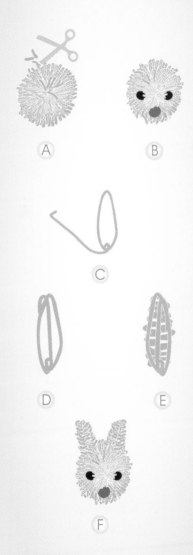

A

B

C

D

E

F

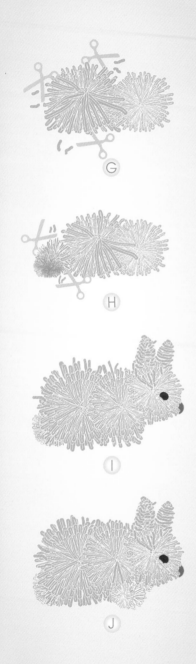

G

H

I

J

★10 Sew the chest to the bottom and trim into a dome shape. G

Feet

★11 Wrap the white fashion yarn 60 times around the small cardboard platform to create a foot pompom. Make a second in the same way.

Tail

★12 Wrap the brown fashion yarn 30 times around the small platform then do the same with the white fashion yarn to create a two-colour pompom **(see page 130)**.

Putting Baby Rabbit together

★13 Sew the tail to Baby Rabbit's bottom with brown yarn, keeping the white part of the tail to the back.

Spider's having a party tonight and I just love to dance!

Carefully trim some of the pile from between the bottom and the tail to separate them. H

★14 Sew the head to the chest with brown yarn. I

★15 Sew the feet to the front of the chest with brown yarn, leaving ½in (12mm) space between them. J

★16 Finally, shape all the pompoms by weaving yarn into any bare patches and trimming stray threads.

Spider, just for this one dance, please do try to keep in step.

47

Spinney Spider has a soft, relaxed design, is easy to make and can be manipulated into fun poses. This un-scary character is a real friend.

Spinney Spider

What you need:

Materials

* 2oz (50g) ball of dark grey yarn
* 2oz (50g) ball of black fashion yarn
* ⅜in (10mm) ready-made black glittery pompoms x 2
* 9 x ³⁄₁₆in (230 x 5mm) black or brown pipe-cleaners x 5
* Black thread

Tools

* Craft scissors
* Sewing needle
* Small cardboard platform **(see page 118)**
* Pencil for shaping foot pods

I find that not many people are afraid of me once they've been over for tea.

Head

★ **1** Wrap the black fashion yarn 70 times around the small cardboard platform then do the same with the grey yarn to make a two-colour pompom **(see page 130)**. Trim away any stray yarn.

Pincers

★ **2** Take half a black or brown pipe-cleaner. Wrap a few layers of grey yarn over the tips. Fold ¼in (6mm) of each tip over and cover with the yarn to blend the folds in. Curl the ends then bend the pipe-cleaner in the middle so that the curled ends face inwards. (A)

Body

★ **3** Wrap the black fashion yarn 80 times around the small cardboard platform then do the same with grey yarn to create another two-colour pompom. Again, trim any stray yarn.

Legs

★ **4** Take a black or brown pipe-cleaner and make a loop in both ends by folding around a pencil.

Twist the ends together to form two rings. These will be the spider's feet. Do the same with three more. Take each leg and bend at the centre and then at the knees. (B)

★ **5** Wrap the grey yarn over the ends of the feet to create toes. Now wrap the yarn across the middle of the feet and continue up the legs. Apply a second layer to the toes and feet so they are thicker. (C)

★ **6** Take two legs and sew them together with grey thread at their central bends. Do the same with the two remaining legs. (D)

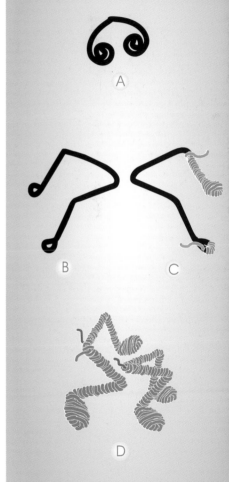

A

B   C

D

49

E

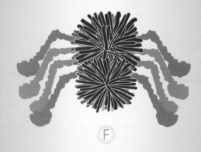

F

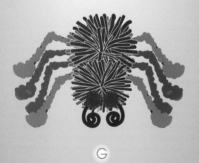

G

7 Now join all the legs at the centre with grey yarn. (E)

Putting Spinney together

8 Sew the head and body together with grey thread. Weave thread through the body a few times to make sure they are secure.

9 Trim the grey sections of the pompoms into circular shapes. Trim the black sections and contour around the bottom,

leaving ½in (12mm) of pile hanging over the bottom grey half. Place the body on top of the legs and sew them together with grey yarn. (F)

10 To finish Spinney Spider, use black thread to sew the pincers into the middle of the head between the grey and black sections and the two ⅜in (10mm) glittery black 'eye' pompoms above the pincers. (G)

Squirrel is easy to make. He is similar to Bud the Mouse and Baby Rabbit but, like Dragonfly Fairy, has a lovely long tail.

Squirrel

What you need:

Materials

* 2oz (50g) ball of brown fashion yarn
* 20z (50g) ball of cream fashion yarn
* ³⁄₁₆in (5mm) black ready-made pompoms x 2
* ³⁄₁₆in (5mm) beige ready-made pompom
* 12 x ³⁄₁₆in (300 x 5mm) beige pipe-cleaners x 3
* Brown thread

* 3 x 1in (75 x 25mm) piece of brown felt

Tools

* Craft scissors
* Yarn needle
* Sewing needle
* Small cardboard platform **(see page 118)**
* Medium cardboard platform **(see page 118)**

Head

1 First of all, wrap the brown fashion yarn 130 times around the small cardboard platform to make a pompom **(see page 129)** and then trim into a head shape. (A)

2 Now cut two ears from brown felt, copying the shape shown in the illustration. Pinch the base of one ear and secure with a couple of stitches. Do the same with the other ear. (B)

3 Sew on the $\frac{3}{16}$in (5mm) black pompoms for eyes and the $\frac{3}{16}$in (5mm) beige pompom for a nose, then sew on the ears. (C)

Body

4 Wrap the brown fashion yarn 60 times around the medium cardboard platform then do the same with the cream fashion yarn to create a two-colour pompom **(see page 130)** for Squirrel's chest.

5 Wrap the brown fashion yarn 100 times around the medium cardboard platform then do the same with cream yarn to form another two-colour pompom for Squirrel's bottom.

6 Sew the chest and bottom pompoms together with brown thread, keeping the white sections of each together and positioning the bottom slightly to one side so that the chest overhangs. (D)

Arms and legs

7 Take two beige pipe-cleaners. Cut both in half then fold them in the middle. Take each piece and loop the ends together. Wrap two pieces with cream yarn for the legs and two pieces with brown yarn for the arms. Cover the hands with contrasting cream yarn and leave the feet unwrapped. (E)

8 Wrap the cream fashion yarn 40 times around the small cardboard platform to make a hind leg pompom. Create another pompom in the same way.

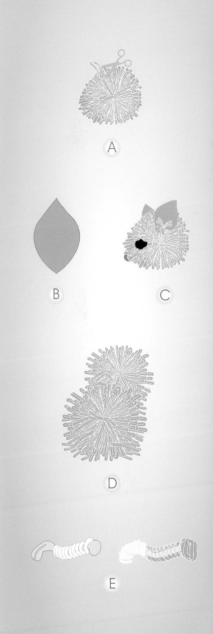

A

B

C

D

E

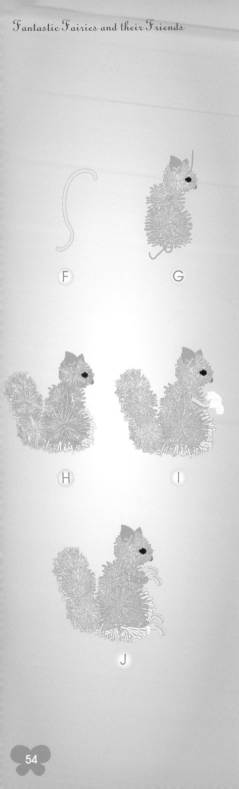

F

G

H

I

J

Tail

9 Wrap the cream fashion yarn 30 times around the small cardboard platform then do the same with the brown yarn to create a two-colour pompom. Make three more in the same way.

10 Take a pipe-cleaner and fold it in half. Loop the ends together. This will form the frame for the tail pompoms. Curve the frame. (F)

Putting Squirrel together

11 Sew the head to the body with brown yarn, setting it slightly forward from the chest. Run the yarn through the three main body pieces to secure them. (G)

12 Sew the tail frame to the bottom of the squirrel with cream yarn. Take the four tail pompoms and place them under the curve of the tail frame, keeping the cream half of each to the back. Sew them to the frame with brown yarn. (H)

13 Sew the arms to the sides of the chest at shoulder level. Weave brown thread through the arms and chest to blend the shoulders and arms into one. (I)

14 Sew the legs to the sides of the bottom with white yarn. Place the hind leg pompoms at the top of each leg and weave white yarn through the pompoms to blend them into the body. (J)

15 To finish, weave yarn into any bare patches and trim uneven threads to balance the shape on all sides.

Fairy Clothes
& Accessories

*This is a favourite party outfit among the fairies and their friends.
Fabulous colours and easy to wear — snip and stitch and they are ready to go!*

Flower Outfit

What you need:

Materials

* Felt in your choice of colours
* Sewing thread to match your fabric
* 1 pipe-cleaner in your choice of colour

Tools

* Craft scissors
* Sewing needle

Most look divine in this outfit, especially me, oh and Bud, and Florabea...

A

B

C

D

E

F

G

5   Layer the flowers (D) and sew them onto a looped pipe-cleaner 'waistband' to create the skirt. (E)

Wristbands

1   Cut a flower from a square of felt measuring 1½in (40mm)

2   Fold the fabric in the centre and then cut out a circle. (F)

3   Now fit over the hands.

Tiara

1   Cut four flowers from 1¼in (30mm) squares of felt.

2   Cut a small circle in the middle of each, following step 2 of Wristbands.

3   Feed a pipe-cleaner through the holes and bend the ends of the pipe-cleaner as shown. (G)

4   Position the tiara on the head of your fairy and connect the pipe-cleaner loops.

Skirt

1   Cut three squares of felt in colours of your choice, measuring 3½in (90mm), 4in (100mm) and 5in (130mm).

2   Cut the three pieces of fabric diagonally and vertically and horizontally, following the white guides on the illustration. (A)

3   Cut curves to shape the petals, again following the white guides. (B)

4   Take each flower, cut in between two of the petals and cut out a circle in the middle. (C)

This is a fantastic seasonal outfit for the fairies and very quick to make. You are just a stitch and a clip away from splendid fun.

Holly Skirt & Tiara

What you need:

Materials
- ✳ Green felt
- ✳ Glittery gold pipe-cleaner
- ✳ ³⁄₁₆in (5mm) glittery red ready-made pompoms x 6
- ✳ ⅛in (3mm) glittery red ready-made pompoms x 6
- ✳ Green thread

Tools
- ✳ Craft scissors
- ✳ Sewing needle

I love getting dressed up for a party!

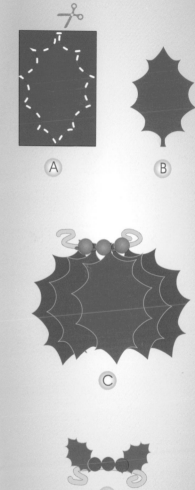

Skirt

⭐ Cut out five holly leaves, each one from a 3½ x 2½in (90 x 65mm) piece of green felt. Ⓐ Ⓑ

⭐ Evenly space on a waist-size looped gold pipe-cleaner and attach with green thread.

⭐ Sew three glittery red 'berries', in the form of small ready-made pompoms, onto the waistband, spacing them ¼in (5mm) apart. Ⓒ

⭐ Place the skirt on the waist of the fairy and connect the looped ends of the pipe-cleaner to secure.

Tiara

⭐ Take a section of gold pipe-cleaner and measure the circumference of your fairy's head. Include enough extra to be able loop the ends of the pipe-cleaner. Cut to fit.

⭐ Sew two small holly leaves at either side of the pipe-cleaner.

⭐ Now sew on three glittery red ³⁄₁₆in (5mm) pompoms between the holly leaves. Ⓓ

⭐ Fasten the tiara around your fairy's head by hooking the looped ends together.

The spooky night cape and hat are easy to make. Grass Sprite loves to wear them with his boots on a cold day. Buggle likes to dress up in them for fun.

Spooky Night Cape & Hat

What you need:

Materials
* Brown felt
* Brown thread

Tools
* Craft scissors
* Sewing needle

A

B

C

D E

Cape

⭐ Cut a cape from a 10in (255mm) square of brown felt following the Spooky Night Cape pattern on **page 149**. Ⓐ

Hat

⭐ Cut out a cone hat top from a 3 x 2½in (75 x 65mm) piece of brown felt Ⓑ and a circular brim from a 2in (50mm) square of brown felt following the Spooky Night Hat pattern on **page 148**. Ⓒ

⭐ Now stitch the long, straight sides of the cone together with matching thread. Ⓓ

⭐ Place the cone over the centre of the brim and stitch round the seam to secure. Ⓔ

Ooh, ahh, where have Buggle's legs gone? It's spooky.

The crown is a fantastic accessory that all the fairies love to wear. It goes especially well with sparkly slippers for a glamorous evening out!

Fairy Crown

What you need:

Materials

* 1 glittery gold or silver pipe-cleaner
* ³⁄₁₆in (5mm) glittery red or white ready-made pompoms x 6
* Thread in a matching colour

Tools

* Sewing needle

We all like to feel special. Wearing a crown does the trick for me, and all my friends too!

★1 Take a full-length pipe-cleaner and shape one end into a circle. (A)

★2 Loop the end and hook it on to the pipe-cleaner to close the circle.

★3 Unloop to zigzag the remaining length into crown spokes. Create six peaks and finish by looping the end through the first peak. (B)

★4 Sew 1/8in (3mm) glittery pompoms on to the peaks of the crown with matching thread. (C)

A

B

C

These sparkly slippers with strapped toes and ankles are perfect for dressing up the fairies and their friends.

Fairy Slippers

Slippers are the most sought-after accessory. I borrowed this pair from Moth.

What you need:

Materials
* 12 x $^1/_{16}$in (300 x 5mm) silver or gold metallic pipe-cleaners x 2

Tools
* Craft scissors

1 Use one full-length pipe-cleaner for each slipper. Make a foot-shaped loop in each using 3in (75mm) at the end of the pipe-cleaners. (A)

2 Close the loops by hooking them onto the pipe-cleaners.

3 Pass the remainder of the pipe-cleaners through the centres of the holes and wrap them once around the ends. You will have now created the soles for each slipper. (B)

4 Next pass the pipe-cleaners around the heels of the slippers and create double-width heel spikes about ½in (12mm) long. (C)

5 Now pass the pipe-cleaners up through the centre of the shoes at the back heels, and make big ankle loops using 1in (25mm) of the pipe-cleaners. (D)

6 Loop the pipe-cleaners down through the centre of the heels to connect the ankle-strap loops. (E)

7 Pass the pipe-cleaners along the soles to the toe areas to fill in the soles some more. (F)

8 Bend the soles of each shoe into a high-heel slipper shape.

9 Pass the pipe-cleaners through the bottom of the slippers to create toe straps. Make semi-circles using about 1in (25mm) of the pipe-cleaners, and adjust the size to fit your fairy's foot. Connect the pipe-cleaners to the other side of the sole of each slipper. (G)

10 Clip any excess pipe-cleaner from the toe straps.

11 The slippers are now ready to fit on to your fairy's feet! (H)

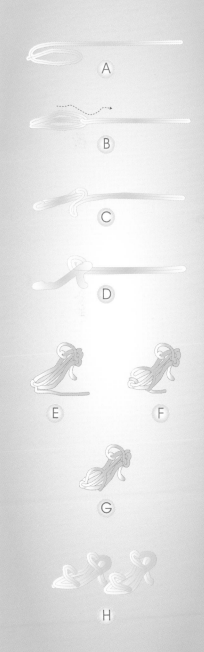

A

B

C

D

E   F

G

H

These felt stitched boots have sides that roll up to any fairy knee or roll down
to cover tiny ankles, making it easy to slip them on and off little feet.

Fairy Boots

What you need:

Materials
* Felt in two bright colours
* Thread in a
  complementary colour

Tools
* Craft scissors
* Needle

Every fairy wants a pair
of these fabulous felt boots.
Especially in orange,
or green, or both!

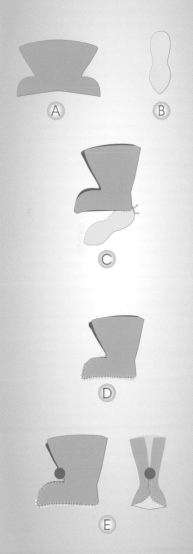

1 Cut a rectangle of brightly coloured felt measuring 6in long by 2in deep (150 x 50mm).

2 Cut the rectangle in half and then cut out a boot shape from both of the pieces. (A)

3 Make the sole of each boot from a different-coloured piece of felt, measuring 2in long by ⅝in high (50 x 15mm). Cut out two sole shapes for each boot. (B)

4 Fold the boots in half to establish the centre of the back.

5 Sew the back of the soles to the bottom of the folds. (C)

6 Stitch the rest of the soles to the bottom of the boots, continuing up past the toes until you reach ankle level. (D)

7 To finish, decorate your boots with a pompom at the last stitch. (E)

Fairy Homes
& Hideaways

The leaf wardrobe has a hinged door and a soft, woven texture. It is a space for holding precious fairy items. Fairies need storage space too!

Leaf Wardrobe

What you need:

Materials

* 2oz (50g) ball of nut-brown yarn
* 12 x ³⁄₁₆in (300 x 5mm) brown pipe-cleaners x 10
* ³⁄₈in (10mm) brown ready-made pompom
* Brown thread

Tools

* Craft needle
* Craft scissors

⭐ 1 To make the door and sides of the wardrobe, curve three full-length pipe-cleaners and connect them to make three circular shapes. Push against the connection points to make three leaf shapes. Ⓐ

⭐ 2 Loop half a pipe-cleaner to the centre of one shape. Ⓑ

⭐ 3 Using brown yarn and a needle, weave across it, using the central post to secure the yarn in the middle. Ⓒ

⭐ 4 Cover the entire shape with yarn in this way. This will form the door of the wardrobe. Ⓓ

⭐ 5 Wrap a pipe-cleaner around the base of one of the remaining shapes and connect it to the base of the other, looping the pipe-cleaner as you go to form feet. Ⓔ

⭐ 6 Now connect the front, sides, and back of the wardrobe with a pipe-cleaner. Ⓕ

⭐ 7 Using four pipe-cleaners, cover the base and middle bars with rows of pipe-cleaners. The middle bars will become shelves. Now connect the top of the wardrobe with half a pipe-cleaner. Ⓖ

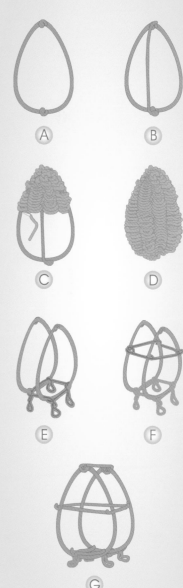

Ⓐ

Ⓑ

Ⓒ

Ⓓ

Ⓔ

Ⓕ

Ⓖ

H

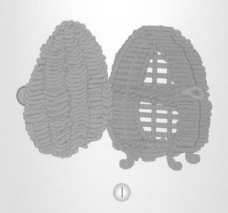

I

I've searched everywhere for my sparkly slippers. Where could they be?

★ 8 Cover the sides of the wardrobe with woven yarn, following the same process as for the door.

★ 9 Cover the back of the wardrobe with a grid pattern. H

★ 10 Attach the door to the front of the wardrobe by weaving a hinge about 1in (25mm) long on one side of the wardrobe and through the corresponding edge of the door.

★ 11 Make a yarn loop latch on the other side of the wardrobe. Finally, using brown thread, sew a ⅜in (10mm) pompom to the door for a handle. I

Fairy Moth, they are in the wardrobe — the first place you should have looked!

This easy-to-make lightweight bed has a soft canopy that curls up to hold pillows in place. It is admired among the fairies for its springy comfort.

Leaf Bed

What you need:

Materials

* ✳ 2oz (50g) ball of brown yarn
* ✳ 12 x ³⁄₁₆in (300 x 5mm) brown pipe-cleaners x 24

Tools

* ✳ Craft needle
* ✳ Craft scissors

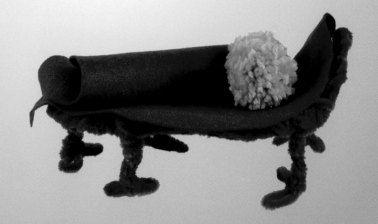

> We have many luxuries — a leaf bed is just one.

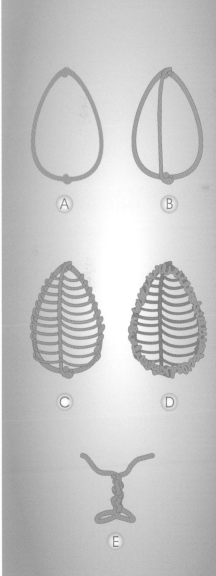

⭐ 1 To make the bed frame, curve two full-length pipe-cleaners and connect them to make a circular shape. Stretch at one end to create a leaf shape. (A)

⭐ 2 Place a pipe-cleaner down the centre of the leaf and attach it by looping it on at both ends. (B)

⭐ 3 Attach 11 pipe-cleaners across the leaf, passing them underneath the central one. Loop the ends around the edges. (C)

⭐ 4 To reinforce the rim of the leaf bed, wrap four full-length pipe-cleaners around it, making a knobbly border. (D)

⭐ 5 Fold a full-length pipe-cleaner in half. Twist both sides together until you reach 1in (25mm) from the ends. Make a big loop at each end. (E)

⭐ 6 Now wrap it around one side of the bed towards the front to form a bed post and foot. Reinforce it by wrapping another pipe-cleaner around it.

⭐ 7 Wrap a third pipe-cleaner through the post to fill in any spaces and smooth out the curly shape then spiral the remainder around the rim of the bed frame, weaving the end into the rim.

(F)

(G)

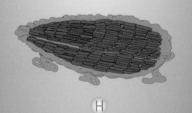

(H)

Ahh, finally! All that flying has made me tired.

⭐ 8 Make four more posts in this way. Position one at the rounded front edge and space the remaining posts so that the leaf bed can stand on a flat surface. (F)

⭐ 9 Using brown yarn, weave around the pipe-cleaners on the base of the bed, from the top pointed end of the frame downward. Secure the yarn onto the pipe-cleaners as you progress down the bed. (G)

⭐ 10 Fill in all the spaces until you have covered the entire surface of the bed. (H)

⭐ 11 Curve the pointed end of the bed upwards by pressing against a tube.

⭐ 12 To dress the bed, make felt 'leaf' blankets following the pattern on **page 148** and pompom pillows following Berry Treasure Bush step 1 on **page 81**.

With long legs like mine, your toes can peep out of the blanket and become cold during the night.

Berry Treasure Chest is loosely woven with a hinged lid and disguised with foliage and berries. It is ideal for hiding small treasures and cheeky fairies.

Berry Treasure Chest

What you need:

Materials

* 12 x $^3/_{16}$in (300 x 5mm) brown pipe-cleaners x 12
* 2oz (50g) ball of spring-green yarn
* 2oz (50g) ball of yellow-green yarn
* $^3/_{16}$in (5mm) berry-red ready-made pompoms x 15

Tools

* Small cardboard platform **(see page 118)**
* Yarn needle

This was an extremely good idea of yours.

1. Combine the two green yarns and wrap the mixed yarn 25 times around the small cardboard platform to make a pompom **(see page 129)**. Make three more in this way.

2. Curve three brown pipe-cleaners into circles, looping the ends to secure them. These will form the rim of the lid, plus the top and bottom rims of the base.

3. Cut eight pipe-cleaners in half. Loop four halves onto one circle, pinching the connections to secure. Cut away any excess pipe-cleaner. This circle will form the lid. Ⓐ

4. Take another circle and loop eight halves onto it, again twisting them to secure. Cut away any excess pipe-cleaner. This will form the base. Ⓑ

5. Make four side support posts by looping the four remaining halves onto the base, two on either side, placing them evenly apart. Connect these posts to the rim. Ⓒ

6. Thread a yarn needle with yellow-green yarn. Weave through the base by wrapping under and over the pipe-cleaner spokes. Cover the entire base in this way.

D

E

F

G

It's great fun being a fairy but all that flying about makes me tired!

★ 7 Continue to weave yarn through the four posts, covering the side walls and rim. D

★ 8 Now cover the lid with woven yarn, too. E

★ 9 Place the pompoms on top of the lid. Loop spring-green yarn through the pompoms to create leafy foliage and to secure them in place. F

★ 10 Weave loops of spring-green yarn across the entire surface of the lid to look like foliage. Fill in any spaces around the edges of the pompoms and weave loops into the rim so that it blends with the base. Cover the sides with loops, too.

★ 11 Attach the lid to the base by weaving a 1in (25mm) hinge into one edge of the lid and base.

★ 12 Finally, sew ³⁄₁₆in (5mm) berry-red pompoms evenly across the sides and lid. G

There are times when you just want to curl up and sleep somewhere cosy.

The grass hut is a cosy space to relax in. Snug walls encircle a comfy base providing cover from the sun.

Grass Hut

What you need:

Materials

✳ 12 x $^3/_{16}$in (300 x 5mm) green pipe-cleaners x 36

Tools

✳ Pencil for shaping the hut entrance 'twists'
✳ Craft scissors

These days, all fashionable gardens have curvy pipe-cleaner designs like this.

84

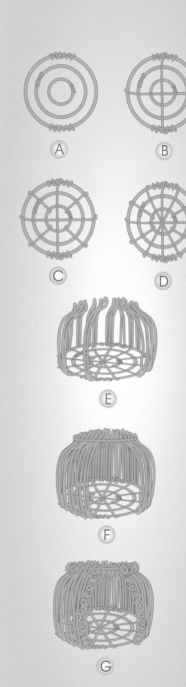

1 The base consists of three circles connected by 'spokes'. To start, connect two curved pipe-cleaners together to create a circle with a 5in (125mm) diameter.

2 Create a second circle using one full-length pipe-cleaner and connecting the looped ends.

3 Create an even smaller circle using half a pipe-cleaner with the ends looped together.

4 Place the three circles inside one another on a table. A

5 Place half a pipe-cleaner through the centre of the circles then loop the ends onto the big circle to make the first spoke. Place another pipe-cleaner the same size across the circle to create a second spoke through the centre of the ring. B

6 Repeat the pattern again, placing two half pipe-cleaners diagonally through the centre of the rings. C

7 Stabilize the middle circle to the outer ring by placing two half pipe-cleaners evenly around the circle to create another cross. Connect by looping the ends together. D

8 Now take 23 full-length pipe-cleaners and fold each in half. Leave a 1in (25mm) straight segment at the tips. Connect them to the circular base by looping the bottom ends onto the outer ring. Position them evenly around the base to make the hut walls but leave one quadrant open for the entrance. E

9 Curve one full-length pipe cleaner, connect the ends to make a circle with a $3\frac{1}{2}$in (90mm) diameter. Gather the tips of the blade walls into the ring. Fold the ends of the blade tips over the ring to secure the blades into a crown at the top of the hut. F

10 To create the entrance 'twists', coil a full-length pipe-cleaner around a pencil. Create one for each side of the entrance. Loop the spiral ends onto the crown ring and base. G

It's traditional to play charades in the grass hut.

H

I

J

K

L

⭐ For the dome lid, create a circle by curving a full-length pipe-cleaner and looping the ends together. Make the diameter slightly larger than the crown ring, so that the lid fits snugly around the folds of the crown blade tips. Curve two half-length pipe-cleaners. Connect them to the lid ring and create a dome shape with a criss-cross pattern. Ⓗ

⭐ Now curve four half-length pipe-cleaners. Weave these curves through the bottom ring to connect to the top crossbar. Make a flower shape with four petals. Curve them to follow the curve of the dome. Ⓘ

⭐ Curve two half-length pipe-cleaners. Fold the middle section in the centre of the loop to make a double petal form. Make two double petal shapes and connect to the top of the dome. Ⓙ

⭐ Finish the dome with a spiral made from half a pipe-cleaner, and then connect it to the top dome petals. Ⓚ

⭐ Finally, place the dome onto the crown. Unfold each 'blade tip' through the dome circle and fold over again to secure. Connect all the blades to the dome ring to secure the shapes in place. Ⓛ

It's a film, a television show and a book. It's got a one-word title and it looks like this!

This big, soft pumpkin has a basket lid and takes some time to make.
It is an ideal fairy sleeping chamber.

Pumpkin Hideaway

What you need:

Materials

* 12 x $3/16$in (300 x 5mm) yellow pipe-cleaners x 19
* 12 x $3/16$in (300 x 5mm) light green pipe-cleaner
* 2oz (50g) ball of green yarn
* 4oz (100g) ball of pale orange chunky yarn
* 4oz (100g) ball of orange yarn
* 2oz (50g) balls of 2-ply golden yellow yarn x 2 or 4oz (100g) ball of 4-ply golden yellow yarn

Optional:

* 6 x 6in (150 x 150mm) felt squares x 2 in leaf colours to make leaf-shaped blankets

Tools

* Craft scissors
* Craft needle
* Small cardboard platform **(see page 118)**

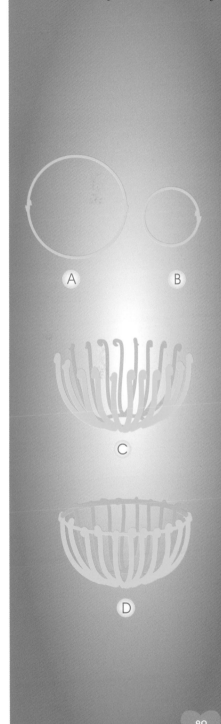

1　Make 72 pompoms from the 2-ply golden yarn, wrapping it 90 times around the cardboard platform.

2　Make 18 smaller pompoms from the same yarn, wrapping it 70 times. Both sets of pompoms will be used to cover the base of the pumpkin.

3　Make 16 even smaller pompoms from the 2-ply golden yarn, wrapping it 60 times. These will be used to line the inside rim of the pumpkin lid.

4　Make one pompom from the 2-ply green yarn, wrapping the yarn 100 times.

5　Make another pompom from the 2-ply green yarn, this time wrapping it 80 times. This pompom and the one you have just made will be used for the stalk.

6　Now curve all 22 pipe-cleaners. Loop both ends of each one, apart from the green pipe-cleaner, which needs to remain unlooped.

7　Take two of the pipe-cleaners and connect the ends to create a circle with a 6in (approx. 150mm) diameter. Ⓐ

8　Make a second smaller circle using one connected pipe-cleaner for the base of the pumpkin. Ⓑ

9　Cut nine full-length pipe-cleaners in half. Hook them onto the large circle, facing them inwards and spacing them evenly apart. Ⓒ

10　Place the small circle in the centre of the large circle and connect the 18 'spokes' to it to create a basket shape. Ⓓ

11　Next, make a lid for the pumpkin by connecting two full-length pipe-cleaners together and creating a circle. Secure the circle by hooking the looped ends together. Adjust the lid circle so that it rests inside but almost touches the edges of the basket.

A   B

C

D

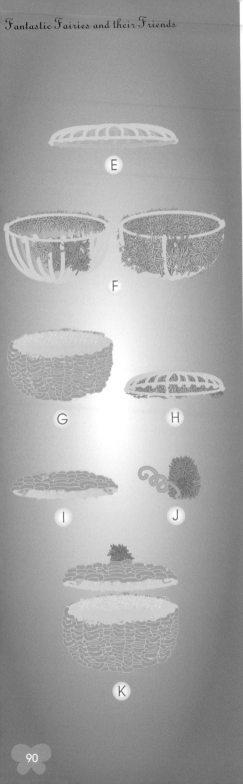

12 To make the top section of the lid create a small circle from half a pipe-cleaner. Next cut five pipe-cleaners into quarters and connect the 18 pieces to the large circle, spacing them evenly. (E)

13 To fill the sides of the pumpkin, sew the 72 golden pompoms around the rim and between all the spokes with matching yarn. Then sew some of the 18 smaller golden pompoms around the base. (F)

14 Now cover the outside of the bowl with a layer of orange yarn. (G)

15 Sew all 16 of the smallest pompoms to the inside and rim of the lid using matching yarn. Cover the lid with golden yarn. (H)

16 Next, using small stitches, sew the remainder of the 18 small golden pompoms onto the top of the lid and rim with orange yarn. (I)

17 Stitch across the pompoms and weave yarn into the spoke cavities to create even channels. Cover the entire surface of the lid with orange yarn, except the circle in the centre of the lid.

18 To make the green stalk sew both of the small green pompoms together using matching yarn. Clip away the top of the stalk to create a flat area and trim the sides to smooth the shape into a tube that widens at the bottom. Place the stalk into the hole in the centre of the lid and sew in place with green yarn. Position a curved green pipe-cleaner at the base of the stalk and wrap it around the stalk. Pull away to release the spiral. Sew into the pompom stalk with green yarn. (J)

19 Finally, apply a second layer of 'skin' to the pumpkin using an alternative shade of orange yarn. Weave into the pumpkin crevasses and maintain the pompom pattern lines. Make sure you keep the lid and base aligned. (K)

The toadstool is an ideal hiding place for small fairies, creatures and accessories. Scatterpillar is particularly fond of it as he loves bright colours!

Toadstool

What you need:

Materials

* 12 x ³⁄₁₆in (300 x 5mm) white pipe-cleaners x 10
* 12 x ³⁄₁₆in (300 x 5mm) red pipe-cleaners x 4
* 4oz (100g) balls of red yarn x 2
* 2oz (50g) ball of green yarn
* 2oz (50g) ball of cream yarn

Tools

* Needle
* Craft scissors
* Small cardborad plolatform (**see page 118**)
* Medium cardboard platform (**see page 118**)

1   Make three or four cream pompoms using the small cardboard platform. Wrap the yarn 100 times.

2   Make eight beige pompoms using the medium cardboard platform. Wrap the yarn 100 times. Alternatively wrap 200 revolutions around the small cardboard platform to make 15 small pompoms.

3   Combine two strands of red yarn, and wrap the doubled yarn 50 times around the small cardboard platform. Create 50 pompoms in this way.

4   Wrap cream yarn 100 times around the small cardboard platform. Make three pompoms in this way.

5   Loop the ends of four red pipe-cleaners and curve each one. Hook two together at one end. Take one end, bring it round and hook it on to create a circle with a 5in (125mm) diameter. This will leave a section that overhangs the circle.

6   Create an arch measuring ¾in (20mm) in height by placing the remaining pipe-cleaner onto the 5in (125mm) ring. This will form the cap hinge and will be woven into the cap with red yarn. (A)

7   Make a cross-shaped dome with the remaining two curves and attach looped ends onto the 5in (125mm) ring. (B)

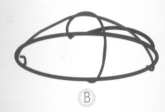

8   Thread a needle with red yarn and pass the yarn through the centre of a red pompom. Knot the end to secure. Wrap the yarn around the frame and reinsert through the pompom. Repeat this once then double knot the yarn and cut off. Insert yarn through a second red pompom and secure at the side of the first in the same way. Repeat until you have covered the frame of the cap. (C)

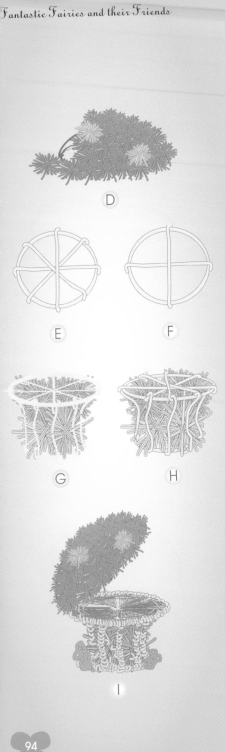

D

E

F

G

H

I

9   Now fill in the spaces with more red pompoms, weaving yarn through new pompoms and into pompoms already in place. Place one or two cream pompoms in each segment of the cap to form markings. Fill in any gaps with red yarn to create an even covering. (D)

10   Make a circle 5in (125mm) in diameter using two white curved pipe-cleaners hooked together. Cut another two in half and use the four pieces to hook onto the circle like wheel spokes. This will create the frame for the top of the stalk. (E)

11   Loop the ends of a white pipe-cleaner together to create a circular base for the stalk. Cut another in half and hook the two pieces onto the circle in a criss-cross shape. (F)

12   Next cut four white pipe-cleaners in half and then hook the eight pieces vertically and evenly spaced onto the base to form the sides of the stalk. Now hook on the circular top. (G)

13   Stuff the centre of the stalk with beige pompoms. Weave beige yarn through the sides and into the pompoms to secure them. Cover the sides with the yarn then wrap and loop it through the stalk to blend it in and make it really solid. (H)

14   Do the same with the circular top of the stalk to cover the flat surface and blend it in with the rest.

15   Using the beige yarn again, connect the cap to the stalk by weaving through the curved hinge. Make sure the cap and the top of the stalk are aligned. Now create 'grass' loops around the base using green yarn. (I)

16   Finally, to smooth the appearance of the cap, use sharp scissors to trim stray threads and weave yarn into any bare patches between the pompoms. An alternative method is to use a lint shaver to smooth the cap quickly and effectively. The stalk has a loose texture, so there is no need to trim it.

After a good workout,
I like to rest in the shade.

This lightweight tree has a secret space at top of its trunk. Its soft, loose texture makes it a wonderful place for fairies to rest or play.

Tree Hideaway

What you need:

Materials

* 9 x ⅛in (230 x 3mm) brown pipe-cleaners x 50
* 12 x ³⁄₁₆in (300 x 5mm) green pipe-cleaners x 6
* 2oz (50g) ball of beige yarn
* 4oz (100g) ball of brown yarn
* 4oz (100g) ball of leaf-green yarn
* 4oz (100g) ball of dark-green yarn

Tools

* Craft scissors
* Craft needle
* Small cardboard platform **(see page 118)**
* Medium cardboard platform **(see page 118)**

1 First make 36 leaf-green pompoms using the small cardboard platform and wrapping the yarn around it 50 times.

2 Next make multi-green pompoms by wrapping the small cardboard platform 25 times with two strands of two shades of green.

3 Now curve five pipe-cleaners. Make two circles, each with a 4in (100mm) diameter, from two of the pipe-cleaners.

4 Next cut one pipe-cleaner in half and hook the two halves onto the first circle, creating a horizontal cross. This will form the base of the tree trunk. (A)

5 Loop the ends of eight pipe-cleaners and hook them on vertically to the base, spacing them evenly around. Take the second circle and place it over the eight pipe-cleaners. The ring can drop to the bottom of the base for now. (B)

6 Make an oval using two curved brown pipe-cleaners looped together. The oval should be 6in (150mm) long by 4in (100mm) wide. Place ten pipe-cleaners horizontally across the oval to create ten evenly spaced lines. Hook the ends on and loop any excess pipe-cleaner around the sides.

7 Now weave five pipe-cleaners under and over the lines to form a grid, again hooking the ends on and wrapping any excess around the sides. (C)

8 Hook the grid onto the eight vertical pipe-cleaners. (D)

9 Wrap beige yarn 150 times around the medium cardboard platform to create a pompom. Make five more in this way. These will cover the top of the tree trunk.

10 Wrap brown yarn 120 times around the small cardboard platform to make a pompom then make 13 more. They will make up the bark.

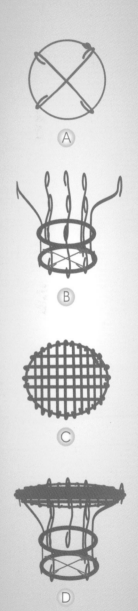

A

B

C

D

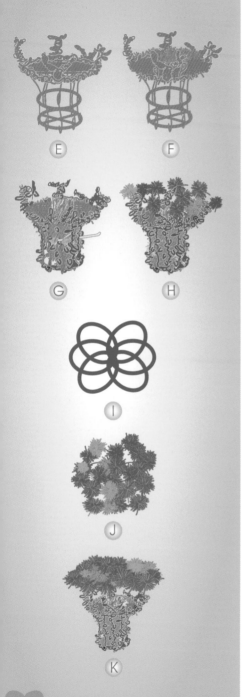

E

F

G

H

I

J

K

11 Build up the side of the grid by weaving pipe-cleaners around the edge of the oval. Create branches by folding and twisting pipe-cleaners around the edge. Wrap more pipe-cleaners around these branches, winding, weaving and twisting them to thicken them. Add as many branches as you like and form them into various shapes. These branches will provide support for the lightweight leaf canopy. (E)

12 Now place a few of the beige pompoms into the centre of the grid and surround them with brown pompoms. Weave thread through the pompoms and onto the grid to secure them. (F)

13 To fill the centre of the tree trunk, place the remaining beige pompoms underneath the centre of the grid and fill the rest with brown pompoms. Sew the remaining brown pompoms down the sides. Weave thread through the sides and base and into the pompoms in the middle to secure them. (G)

14 Now weave thread onto the inside edge of the grid and leave the beige yarn to peek through the grid like a carpet. Wrap the branches with brown thread and pass thread through them. Tip each branch with either a mottled green or plain green pompom. (H)

15 For the leaf canopy, curve six green pipe-cleaners. Loop the ends of one to create a circle. Insert a second pipe-cleaner through the first and loop the ends to make a second attached circle. Create more circles, inserting them and connecting them to the first two rings to create a canopy shape. Sew the circles together with green yarn to make the canopy more sturdy and to create a subtle arc. (I)

16 Sew the green pompoms on top of the canopy, positioning some together, some higher than others and leaving some spaces. (J)

17 Trim stray threads then place the canopy on top of the tree. (K)

Curves and more curves make up this elegant throne. At garden parties Fairy Empress lets her friends use it.

Grass Throne

What you need:

Materials

* 12 x ³⁄₁₆in (300 x 5mm) green pipe-cleaners x 26
* 12 x ³⁄₁₆in (300 x 5mm) yellow pipe-cleaners x 2
* Green thread
* **Optional decoration:** 1 yellow glittery ready-made pompom, pink felt and plain yellow ready-made pompoms

Tools

* Sewing needle
* Craft scissors

★ 1 To make the canopy, begin by creating six circles, each from a green pipe-cleaner. Ⓐ

★ 2 Sew two sets of circles together with green thread. Ⓑ

★ 3 Place one set on top of the other set to form a criss-cross. Unloop the second set of circles and weave them through the first set. Reconnect the circles so that the shape is secure. Now curve the criss-cross into a canopy shape. Ⓒ

★ 4 Take the remaining set of circles and connect these to the criss-cross in the same way to form a six-petal flower shape.

★ 5 Weave a green pipe-cleaner through the top of the dome and then link the two ends together to form a circle. This will reinforce the dome shape. Ⓓ

★ 6 To finish the edge of the shape, cut three green pipe-cleaners in half and curve each piece. Use them to connect the petals together. Ⓔ

★ 7 To make the throne base, loop two curved green pipe-cleaners together, forming a circle that is 6in (150mm) in diameter. Ⓕ

★ 8 To make the pattern in the base circle, curve three full-length green pipe-cleaners then cut them in half. Place the first curved pipe-cleaner into the centre of the circle and connect each end to the sides to create an arc through the centre. Ⓖ

★ 9 Do the same with the other five pieces of pipe-cleaner, positioning them evenly around the circle to create a triangular pattern. Ⓗ

101

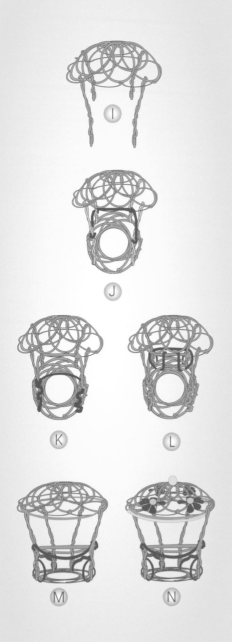

10 Now connect the canopy to the base by threading four folded pipe-cleaners through the canopy petal connections. Place them evenly around the perimeter. Twist the folded stems together to secure the post connection. Ⓘ

11 Next connect the ends of the four posts through the outer ring of the base.

12 Wind a pipe-cleaner around the sides and the back of the posts to create the back shape of the bench outline. Ⓙ

13 Add a curved pipe-cleaner to the middle of the canopy to create the inside of the bench. Connect the sides of the pipe-cleaner to the front posts. Twist the remaining sections around the front posts to blend. Ⓚ

14 Loop the end of one pipe-cleaner over the back curve of the bench at one side. Make a straight crossbar down to connect both of the bench arches. Ⓛ

15 Fold the pipe-cleaner around the back post to create a second curve at the back of the bench. Weave the pipe-cleaner through the second back post under the front bench arc and fold over the top of the bar to make a second crossbar. The open space between the bench crossbars is the fairy bottom dip. The open space above the bench between the bench posts provides support to fairy wings. Ⓜ

16 Lastly, weave two curved yellow pipe-cleaners through the posts and rings to trim the canopy rim and then decorate, if you wish, with flowers, and a yellow glittery pompom. Ⓝ

We try not to fight over this but Ladybug knows, it's my turn on the throne. Oh well, I have the crown.

The flower sceptre is an elegant accessory. It is used to make a statement at grand public occasions.

Flower Sceptre

What you need:

Materials

✳ 12 x ³⁄₁₆in (300 x 5mm) green pipe-cleaners x 4
✳ ³⁄₈in (10mm) purple ready-made pompom
✳ 2in (50mm) square of pink felt

Tools

✳ Sewing needle
✳ Craft scissors

> *I waited, and waited. Eventually I plucked up the courage to talk to the flower but it didn't talk back!*

1 Fold a full-length pipe-cleaner in half then make a leaf-shaped loop using 2in (50mm) of the end. Do the same with two more pipe-cleaners. Ⓐ

2 Wrap and twist the six 'stalks' together, to make a sturdy pole and then fan out the three leaf loops to make a stable base. Ⓑ

3 Loop the ends of three of the stalks to make leaf shapes, using 2in (50mm) of pipe-cleaner for each. You will be left with three straight stalks in the middle. Ⓒ

4 Take another pipe-cleaner and fold it in half. Wrap it around the three straight stalks. Ⓓ

5 Create a back for the flower head by making 1in (25mm) loops with both ends of the fourth pipe-cleaner. Curl the ends of the remaining stalks. Ⓔ

6 Cut a pink flower from a 2in (50mm) square of felt. Sew a ⅜in (10mm) purple pompom in the centre with sewing thread. Now sew the flower head to the top of the stalk to finish your flower sceptre. Ⓕ

Mouse's sought-after chariot is used for special occasions and keeping fit. All seek to recline on the sleek, cosy seat and glide across the countryside.

Grass Blade Chariot

Bud is the fittest mouse around.

What you need:

Materials
* 12 x ³⁄₁₆in (300 x 5mm) green pipe-cleaners x 17

Tools
* Craft scissors

1. Use half a straight pipe-cleaner for the back crossbar of the seat. Use another half to make a curve for the front of the seat. Loop the curved pipe-cleaner onto the back bar, spacing it 2in (50mm) apart. (A)

2. Next take a full-length curved pipe-cleaner to build the back frame and seat bars. Place the curve onto the crossbar, position it $\frac{1}{2}$in (12mm) down from the top outside curve. (B)

3. Wrap the pipe-cleaner around the back crossbar and loop the remaining straight section onto the front curve of the seat to make bench bars. (C)

4. Attach another curved pipe-cleaner and create the second back seat ring. Position in the centre of the back of the seat curve and connect the inner curve to the crossbar and front bench. Fold the remaining strips under the front curve of the seat. (D)

5. Repeat the step above for a third back seat ring. (E)

6. To secure the back and bottom of the seat together, weave a folded full-length pipe-cleaner through the centre of the three rings. Fold the remaining section over the top of the front of the chair and attach it to the front curve to create a bench bar in the middle of the seat. Loop the ends onto the front curve. (F)

7. Curve two more full-length pipe-cleaners. Weave them on either side of the central back bar and loop onto the seat in the same way. The seat will have ten bench bars when all three bars are connected to the back of the seat. (G)

8. Now take two full-length pipe-cleaners to make two armrests. Fold them around the outer ring, one on each side, under the left and right curved back bars you have just made. They will protrude through the back of the chair. Curve them then attach the ends on either side to the front of the seat. (H)

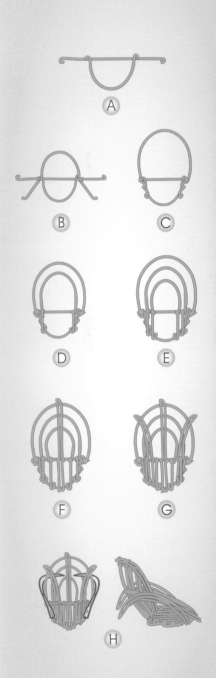

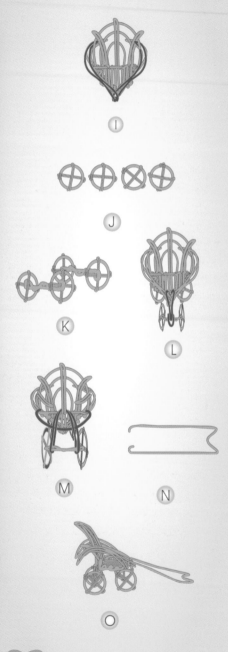

I

J

K

L

M

N

O

9   Create a second layer for the armrests. Fold a full-length pipe-cleaner in half and curve. Weave the folded end through the back of the left armrest bar. Connect the end of the fold onto the outer ring, and arc the remaining section around the side. Attach to the front by placing the armrest bar into the centre of the seat. Weave a second curved stem through the right armrest bar to match the design on the other side. (I)

10   To make the chariot wheels, take half a pipe-cleaner and curve to make a small circle. Loop to close. Make four circles in this way. Place two spokes on each wheel using $1/4$in (5mm) of a pipe-cleaner to create crossbars. (J)

11   To make the wheel axis, fold half a pipe-cleaner and twist into a solid bar. Connect a wheel to the end loops and pinch the twisted bar onto the central cross of the wheel spokes. Attach wheels to both sides of the bar. (K)

12   To attach the front wheels to the chariot, curve a full-length pipe-cleaner and fold in half. Loop the ends onto the seat between the armrest bars. Fold the long loop strip around the wheel axis. Fold the loop around the bar to secure the wheel axis. Leave room for the wheel bar to spin around the connection. (L)

13   To make the back wheel section, curve half a pipe-cleaner and loop it onto the back of the seat. Fold a full-length pipe-cleaner in half and weave it through the central bar at the backrest. Connect the ends to the back wheel bar. (M)

14   Create the chariot harness with a full-length pipe-cleaner. Make a long 'M' shape with loops at the bottom. (N)

15   Lastly, attach the harness to the front of the chariot, hooking the looped ends onto the left and right armrests. (O)

Petal dresses are all the rage this season, Florabea.

Creating your
Fairy World

Sometimes,
I get tongue-tied
when I have to talk
to bigger fairies.

What you Need

Yarn

4-ply yarn in natural, synthetic and fashion thread has been used for many of the projects. The projects incorporate yarn in different ways, including wrapping, weaving, embroidering and sewing. Yarns wrapped onto fingers and cards make up multi-coloured pompom designs, with blocks and bands of colour, or single-colour spheres. Yarn embroidered through wrapped pipe-cleaners and hand-made pompoms creates specific details and features.

Three-dimensionally woven yarn can be passed through pompoms and helps bind model components together and reinforce structures.

Plastic sheets

Translucent plastic sheets, needed to make fairy wings, are available from various sources, including recycled packaged goods, and tags and folders purchased from stationery stores. Stencil-making sheets, which are available in craft stores are also ideal for making fairy wings.

Choose sheets that are difficult to tear, and can take a coloured design. Slightly textured plastic sheets will take pencil colour or crayons. For thin, non-textured, translucent plastic sheeting, use permanent markers. Plastic sheets will not absorb water-based art materials like acrylic paint. Thicker plastic sheets can be engraved with a hand-held engraving device.

Hint: The metal tips at the ends of pipe-cleaners are sharp.

It is best to fold them over (using fingers or pliers) or wrap them with yarn.

Glue

Glue is not required and should not be used. Gluing any part of the project will damage the fabric. All the projects are assembled either by sewing elements together, looping pipe-cleaners together or binding with yarn. The advantage is that projects can be altered, repositioned and parts can be recycled if they are not suitable.

A Felt

Felt is a wonderful material to work with. It comes in a wide variety of colours and is easy to cut with scissors. It requires no hemming, as it does not unravel. Embroidery and sewing thread pass through felt fibres with ease. The coarseness of the material gives substance and enhances the finished appearance and texture of the garment.

B Pipe-cleaners

Pipe-cleaners are wire twisted with chenille or cotton pile. They are available from a variety of craft retailers in vivid colours and can be trimmed, looped, bent, curled, zigzagged or twisted. They are available in various gauges from regular to chunky and bumpy, and can be plain, flecked, glittery, striped and metallic. Chenille-covered pipe-cleaners, or chenille stems as they are also known, are my preferred choice, as the pile is slightly easier to trim, plus they tend to be longer than cotton-covered pipe-cleaners.

C Embroidery thread

Embroidery thread is used to connect commercially made pompoms and pipe-cleaners, along with sewing thread.

Embroidery thread is preferable as it can be separated into individual strands and is more economical to purchase in multi-colour packs than individual spools of sewing thread.

D Pompoms

You will need to make pompoms for many of the projects. How to do this is explained fully on **pages 127–131**. Commercially manufactured pompoms are ideal for tiny items. Pompoms as small as $\frac{1}{8}$in (3mm) are required for fairy noses, eyeballs and decorating. Some fairies are sewn together using $\frac{3}{16}$in (5mm) pompoms for arms and legs. Larger pompoms and embroidered lumps can be used for larger parts. Commercially made pompoms are available in metallic, glittery and solid colours, and are sold by their diameter in packets.

A

B

C

D

115

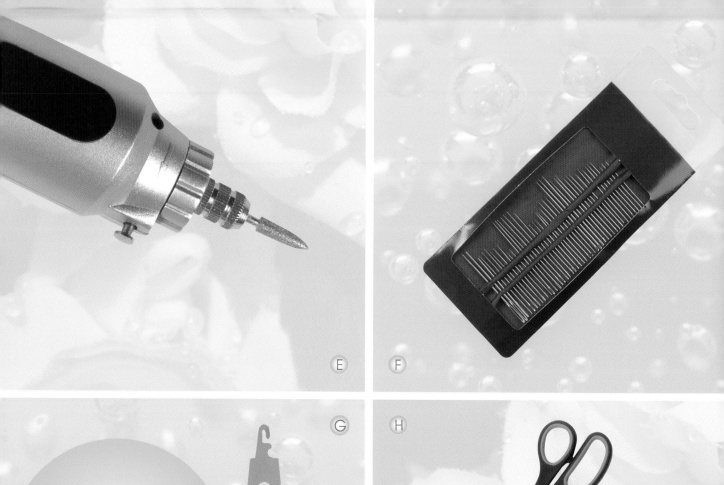

E

F

G

This needle-threader looks uncannily like an umbrella.

H

1

2

3

116

Hint: Keep project tools in a pencil case separate from other similar household items.

Tools should be grease-free if being kept with yarn and material fibres.

E Engraver

This can be used to engrave patterns into wings, which can then be coloured (see Coloured pencils/permanent marker, **page 118)**.

F Needles

Select yarn or darning needles in various lengths and eye widths, equivalent to assorted yarn gauges. Sewing needles are used when connecting $\frac{1}{8}$in (3mm) eyeball pompoms and felt fabric items. Commercially made pompoms have fine fibres and so a finer gauge sewing needle is preferable.

G Needle threader

This item saves time when threading fashion yarn into needles. They are also helpful for younger children.

H Craft or sewing scissors

Craft scissors are useful for cutting felt fabric patterns, clipping yarn, sewing thread and carving designs into pompom shapes. Lightweight craft scissors with rubber handles

and sharp blades with pointed tips are preferable to round-tipped craft scissors. Sharp craft scissors are also required for cutting wing shapes with a smooth clean edge; these scissors should be kept separate and not used for cutting fabric.

1 Utility scissors

General all-purpose scissors are useful for cutting pipe-cleaners, plastic wing shapes and cardboard pompom discs.

2 Pinking shears

Pinking shears cut a zigzag pattern into cloth and can be used to create a decorative effect or to prevent fabric unravelling. They are specifically designed for cutting cloth and should not be used for cutting paper, pipe-cleaner wire or plastic sheets.

3 Embroidery scissors

These are lightweight scissors with sharp precision tips. They are essential for shaping and carving facial features and for fine-tuning the designs.

Quality and care of your scissors

Do not use designated craft and embroidery scissors for anything other than making pompoms, cutting yarn, thread or felt fabric, ribbons and lace. Scissor blades will become dull if used for cutting plastic sheets, paper, pipe-cleaner wire and cardboard.

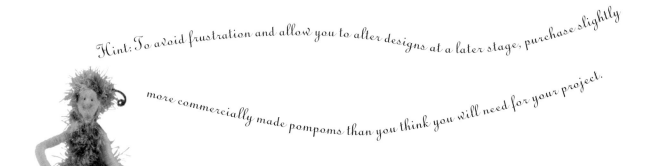

Hint: To avoid frustration and allow you to alter designs at a later stage, purchase slightly more commercially made pompoms than you think you will need for your project.

I Cardboard platforms for wrapping pompoms

Corrugated cardboard, cut into two platform shapes, in sizes small and medium have been used for many of the projects.

How to make cardboard platforms

To make a small cardboard platform, cut three strips of card measuring 1¼ x 3in (32 x 76mm). Stack all three pieces together and tape into a block shape. Cover with sticky tape to secure the fold and make the surface slippery so that the yarn slips off the card. For a medium-sized platform cut a

cardboard strip measuring 2 x 10in (50 x 255mm) and fold it twice equidistantly to make one card. Cover with sticky tape.

Hands and fingers!

The pompoms for the characters and models in this book can also be made by wrapping yarn onto your fingers, rather than onto cardboard platforms (explained fully on page 129).

J Sewing thread

Sewing thread or embroidery thread are used to connect commercially made pompoms and pipe-cleaners. White thread is the best colour to purchase, as it will blend with most commercially manufactured pompoms. Have a broad selection of colours to hand to make up fairies and characters.

K Coloured pencils/ permanent marker

Coloured pencils can be used to draw patterns and colour in wing designs. Pencil crayon colour will rub away with a damp cloth. The colour will remain in engraved design channels, but can be cleaned away with a scouring sponge. Be careful not to abrade the plastic sheet when removing the pencil colours.

L Scissor sharpener

This tool is needed if your craft or utility scissors have become blunt.

Clothes lint shaver (optional)

This can be used as a speedy way to smooth pompom shapes, such as the toadstool project on page 92.

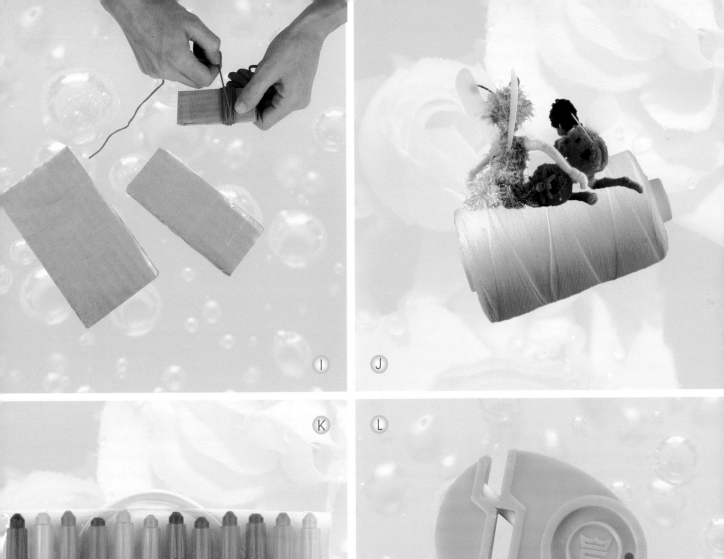

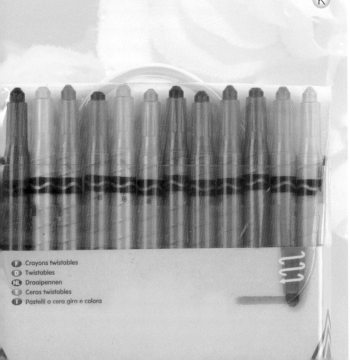

🇫 Crayons twistables
🇩 Twistables
🇳🇱 Draaipennen
🇪 Ceras twistables
🇮🇹 Pastelli a cera gira e colora

Slippers made
from real Italian
pipe-cleaners.
Fantastic!

Working with Pipe-cleaners

Pipe-cleaners are wonderful to work with. They have a colourful fabric crust which can be trimmed with scissors to create features such as wrists and ankles. Because they are so bendy they can be manipulated into any imaginable shape, and they can also be wrapped with yarn.

I get bent out of shape if I don't eat my breakfast.

121

Curving

Use your finger and thumb to pinch the end of a pipe-cleaner. Keeping a grasp on the pipe-cleaner with finger and thumb together, pull against the entire length with an arching tension. This will give the pipe-cleaner a curved shape and is instrumental for making circles, arches and oval shapes. Ⓐ–Ⓒ

Wrapping pipe-cleaners

Pipe-cleaners can be wrapped with yarn to strengthen them, create specific details and body shapes, and also enhance appearance and tactile quality. It is a good way to weave and bind pipe-cleaners together, too. Pipe-cleaners positioned at any angle or shape can be bound with yarn. Ⓓ–Ⓕ

Looping

Use your finger and thumb to pinch the end of a pipe-cleaner. Rotate thumb and finger into a small circle. Ⓖ Do the same at the other end to create loops that can hook or connect pipe-cleaners together.

Closing loops

Pinch the loops to close off the sharp metal ends.

Connecting pipe-cleaners

Connect pipe-cleaners by overlapping loops and then pinch to close. Ⓗ

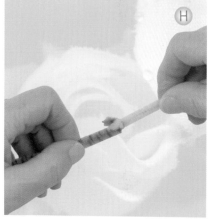

We love pipe-cleaners!

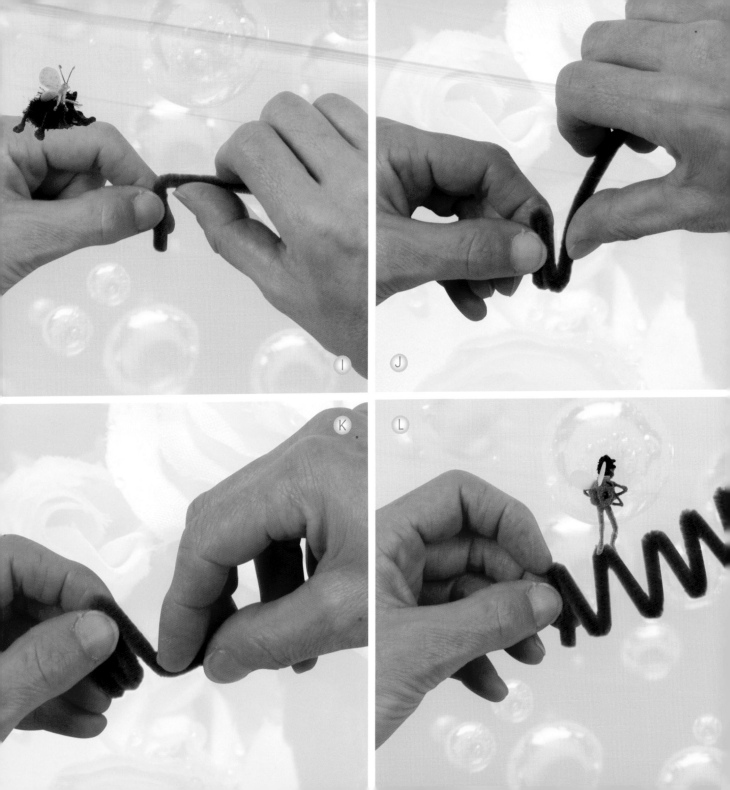

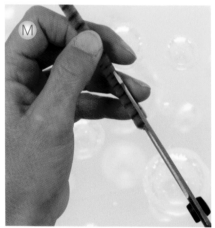

Zigzags

Folding pipe-cleaners abruptly in evenly measured intervals will produce a zigzag pattern. (I)-(L)

Clipping pipe-cleaners

Embroidery or sharp craft scissors can be used to clip sections of pile from pipe-cleaners. Chenille-covered pipe-cleaners are more suitable for this, as those covered in cotton are slightly resistant to the process. (M)-(N)

Take a pipe-cleaner and shape it as desired. Fine-tune the details by clipping away pile from the surface of the pipe-cleaner. Work in stages and apply the same process to duplicate pieces, for example shape ankles, wrists or elbows at the same time so that they match. Antennae, legs and arms involve the clipping process.

Embroidered lumps

Embroider lumps on pipe-cleaners to create muscle on arms and legs and fine detailing like toes, thumbs, elbows and knees. These can easily be added and seamlessly disappear into the wrapping and weaving process to give a life-like appearance to the models.

My mother always made her own.

Making Pompoms

Making pompoms with discs

Although discs are readily available I do not recommend them, which is why they are not mentioned in 'What You Need'. Pompom discs limit you to making pompoms in the sizes of the discs available, and although the projects can be made with the commercially available small and medium plastic discs, they have actually been created with the finger- or card-wrapping technique. If you prefer to use them, though, instructions are given here.

⭐ Thread a large-eyed darning needle with a long length of yarn. Take two discs and, holding them together, wrap the yarn around both of them through the hole in the discs. Wrap until you have covered the entire circumference of the discs and continue as desired – the thicker the layer of yarn the more dense the pompom. New colours can be brought in as desired.

⭐ Now cut around the circumference between the two discs and, with the discs still in place, insert a length of yarn between them. Secure with a firm knot. Remove the discs and trim the pompom as required.

Making pompoms with fingers or cardboard platforms

Making pompoms by wrapping yarn around your fingers or a cardboard platform is more versatile and faster than disc wrapping. It is possible to blend yarns together such as fashion yarn with plain or textured yarn, and make pompoms in various sizes, from very small to very large.

⭐ 1 Secure a length of yarn against your first finger and wrap the yarn around your first and middle fingers (A), or alternatively around your cardboard platform. Continue wrapping, counting each full revolution as you do so. (B)-(C)

⭐ 2 Cut the yarn (D) and remove it by gently pushing the thread off the cardboard or down to the end of your fingers and onto a surface. (E)

⭐ 3 Take a piece of thread, approximately 12in (305mm) and double it over then place it under the mass of thread, being careful not to

separate the loops (F). Tie the doubled-over thread tightly around the mass of loops (G) then tie it again on the opposite side. (H)

⭐ 4 Cut through the loops on either side of the tied thread (I)-(J) then separate the strands and trim the pompom to shape. (K)-(L)

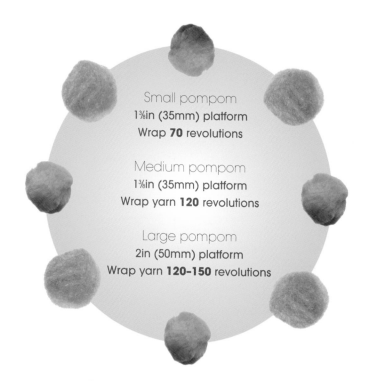

Small pompom
1⅜in (35mm) platform
Wrap **70** revolutions

Medium pompom
1⅜in (35mm) platform
Wrap yarn **120** revolutions

Large pompom
2in (50mm) platform
Wrap yarn **120–150** revolutions

Size of pompom

The number of times you wrap your yarn determines the density, and the width of the platform or size of your fingers determines the final size. The projects mostly incorporate two sizes of pompom: small and medium. There are slight variations in wrapping formulas to create subtle differences in body shapes and parts. Note that 2-ply yarn may require more wraps than 4-ply.

Variegated pompoms

Take two balls of yarn in different colours. Place both strings together then begin to wrap over fingers or top of platform with an even tension. Try not to cross yarn colours over. Apply yarn evenly from side to side, covering about 1in (25mm) in width. (See **page 128** for step-by-step photographs.)

Two-colour pompoms

Colours wrapped together in blocks create pompoms with distinct colour bands. For two-colour pompoms, divide in half the number of times you will wrap the finished pompom. If the total pompom size is 60 revolutions, apply 30 revolutions of the first colour, then place the remaining 30 revolutions of the second colour next to the first band. Wrap the yarn tightly, keeping the colour bands separate. Overlapping thread will create blotches of colour in adjacent colour bands on the finished pompom. (A)–(H)

Spot-colour pompoms

Single-colour pompoms can be decorated with spots of colour, by weaving clusters of different yarn through the core of the pompom area. (I)–(L)

Building up areas

Building up specific areas of the pompom follows the same process as the spot-colour pompom technique. Apply additional thread to patchy areas by weaving a needle through the bare area, then cut the added thread down so it's level with the pompom.

Shaping pompoms

Pompoms are shaped by trimming or carving with scissors, weaving and adding threads to bare areas, and sewing pompoms together to create larger forms.

Hint: Doubling up on yarn will reduce the number of revolutions. For example, a medium pompom takes 70 revolutions, but by using two strings of yarn, only 35 revolutions are necessary.

I don't know which one of us looks grander in our crowns.

> *I'm really looking forward to our Moon Dance Festival.*

Leg Types

> *Dance lessons have helped us.*

Type 1

⭐ Take one pipe-cleaner and make a loop of approximately 1½in (35mm) at one end. This will form a foot. Connect the foot loop by pinching the folded end onto the wire **(see page 135)**. Ⓐ

⭐ Make a small circle just above the connection by twisting the pipe-cleaner into a little loop around a pencil tip. This will form the ankle section.

133

3　Take another pipe-cleaner (I will refer to it as the contour pipe-cleaner) and make a loop of about ½in (12mm) at one end. Connect this to the toe end of the foot loop. Bring the contour pipe-cleaner across the foot and wrap it around the ankle section just above the circle. This connects the instep to the foot. (B)

4　To make the shin and knee, create an arc that is about ½in (12mm) deep with the contour pipe-cleaner. Twist it onto the back part of the leg and create a knee joint 2in (50mm) from the bottom of the ankle. (Maintain the arc in the middle of the shin before twisting the pipe-cleaner at the knee joint.) (C)

5　To create the thigh area, make another arc about ½in (12mm) deep with the contour pipe-cleaner above the knee. Twist it to connect it onto the straight pipe-cleaner, about 2½in (65mm) up from the knee. Twist the contour pipe-cleaner onto the crotch region to fasten. (D)

It must be difficult finding shoes for all those feet Spinney. I know I have to compromise when looking for gloves.

I give up, I can't move.

6　There will be two pieces of pipe-cleaner at the top crotch twist that make half of the tail section. One remnant will be longer than the other. Either remnant can be used for the tail. The longer strip can be used to create the Dragonfly Fairy tail **(see page 22)**. The shorter tail strips are used for the Grass Sprite **(see page 14)**. Clip off one tail segment so that they match in length. Now leave the tail until the second leg is complete.

7　Make the second leg in the same way and cut the tail segments to match those on the first leg. (E)

8　Twist the tail segments together and fold over the sharp tips. (F)

Type 1

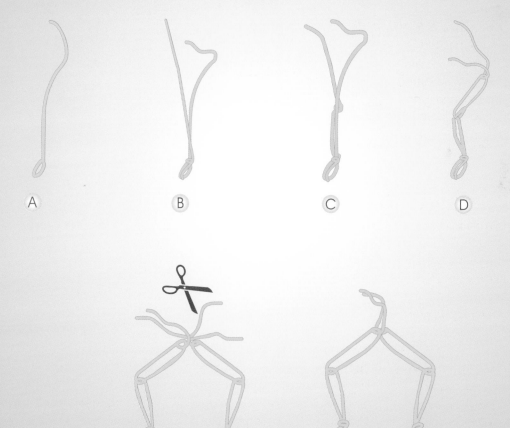

Hint: The secret to a smooth skin finish is to keep layers of thread even and close to each other. Move up and down the figure as you sew in even lines, trying not to cross threads over.

G

H

I

J

Yes, some are blessed with beautiful legs, but we're all different and special in our own way.

10 Now embroider lumps at the back of the leg arc to shape calf muscles. Wrap over the embroidery with a layer of thread. Make knees by applying layers of stitches then cover the knee areas with even layers of wrapped yarn. Pull the thread taught just above knees to create a small indent between the knee and thigh region. (H)

11 Cover the thigh area by applying yarn to the thigh arches and then wrap the tail. Finish wrapping by tapering the yarn at the centre of the crotch region. (I)

12 Once the legs and tail are completely covered, apply another layer of thread to flesh out the tail section, another layer of yarn to cover the legs and feet then highlight knees and lumpy areas with extra layers of thread. (J)

Wrapping the tail and legs

9 Thread a yarn needle with double strands of flesh-coloured yarn. Start at the toe region of the feet. Place yarn through the feet loops and cover the rounded tips with thread. Tug at the yarn and make sure that the thread is distributed evenly over the toe arcs. Draw the craft needle and yarn over the edges of the feet and wrap with a layer of thread. Embroider thread through the instep area to build up an arch shape at the top of the feet. Continue to wrap thread over the lumps of the heels to incorporate them into the feet and blend the seams. Continue to wrap thread to cover the ankle sections then follow the contours of the legs. (G)

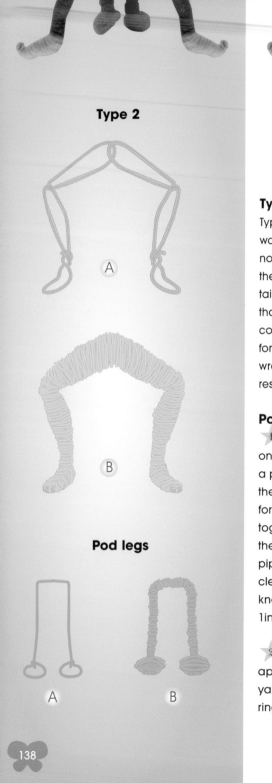

Type 2

Type 2

Type 2 legs are made in the same way as Type 1 except that they're not joined by a tail. The remnants of the pipe-cleaner that created the tail for Type 1 are clipped away so that you can shape leg loops that connect the two legs together and form a crotch area which is then wrapped with yarn along with the rest of the legs. (A)-(B)

Pod legs

1 Take a pipe-cleaner and bend one end over the circumference of a pencil. Foot size is determined by the size of the pencil or tube used to form the foot shape. Twist the wire together to make a small ring. Do the same at the other end of the pipe-cleaner then bend the pipe-cleaner in half. You can also make knees by bending each leg about 1in (25mm) above the feet. (A)

2 Thread a craft needle with the appropriate colour and loop the yarn several times through the small ring to create a toe.

I look really cute up here.

3 Wrap outside of the ring to cover the sides of the foot. Continue to cover the entire surface of the foot. Repeat the same procedure on the other foot by applying yarn to the toe first then moving along the outside of the foot.

4 The spindly legs can be covered with three layers of yarn. The first layer covers the toes, feet and leg section of the pipe-cleaner. Spread the wrapping evenly across the entire pipe-cleaner before moving on to the second layer to the feet, not the toe area, and continue the yarn cover over the whole leg.

5 Finally, cover the legs and feet with a third layer of yarn to smooth out the texture. (B)

Sometimes Bud likes to take long breaks at the most inconvenient times!

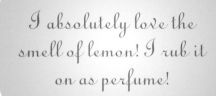

I absolutely love the smell of lemon! I rub it on as perfume!

Arm Types

Type 1

1 Take a full-length pipe-cleaner and fold one tip at 1½in (38mm) from the end to make a palm-shaped loop. You can use a pen or pencil to guide the pipe-cleaner into shape. Hook the loop onto the pipe-cleaner. Create a thumb shape by folding ¼in (5mm) of the palm loop into a thumb bud at the side of the palm **(see page 143)**. Ⓐ

2 Form a second hand and thumb at the other end of the pipe-cleaner. Make sure that the thumbs are pointing in the right directions.

3 Create muscle arches above the hands by joining the tip of a full-length pipe-cleaner onto the wrist area. Make a slight arch then twist it onto the elbow area about 1½in (38mm) up from the wrist. Ⓑ

4 Create a second arch above the elbow then twist around the shoulder area about 1½in (38mm) from the elbow. Ⓒ

5 Duplicate the same arches on the opposite side of the arm and then finish the shape by twisting the tip of the pipe-cleaner onto the second arm above the wrist and clip excess strip **(see page 143)**. Ⓓ

Type 2

1. Use a full-length pipe-cleaner for each arm. Follow the instructions for step 1 of Type 1 arms on the previous page then make a shoulder loop folding the pipe-cleaner in half and looping the tip onto the wrist. Repeat for a second arm. (A)

2. Twist the loop at the elbow to shape and secure muscle arches. Do the same for the other arm. (B)

Wrapping both arm types

1. Wrap the palm loops by placing a needle and yarn through the centres and then passing it around the palms. Anchor thread through the thumb folds to define the thumb shapes. (A)

2. Now wrap yarn across the palms until they are covered and then apply a second layer. (B)

3. Next wrap the wrists with yarn and pull the thread taught to create wrist indentations.

Continue to wrap the length of the arms.

4. When you have wrapped all around the arms, cover them with a another layer of yarn, passing the yarn across the width of the arms.

5. Create muscle definition by embroidering lumps onto the forearms and above the elbows. Wrap yarn over these areas to blend them in. Lastly, apply another layer of yarn to smooth out imperfections and crevasses. (C)

Hurry Bud! I want to be the first to get there!

Type 1

A   B   C

Type 2

A   B

Wrapping arms

A   B   C

Arm pods with hand loops

A   B   C   D

Arm pods with hand loops and thumbs

A

Arm pods with pod hands

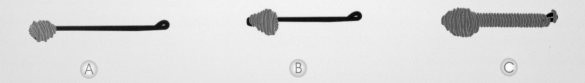

A   B   C

Arm Pods

With hand loops

⭐ 1 Take a 7in (178mm) length of pipe-cleaner and fold the ends around a thin tube like a pencil or chopstick to make a small ring shape. Twist against the tube to bind the rings. Cut in the centre of the pipe-cleaner to separate the arms. Create loops on the ends of the arms to connect thread through body pompoms. Ⓐ

⭐ 2 Wrap the end of each hand with yarn to create fingers. Ⓑ

⭐ 3 Wrap yarn across the palm of each hand. Ⓒ

⭐ 4 Wrap yarn up each arm. Ⓓ

With hand loops and thumbs

To add thumbs, follow the instructions for pod arms with hand loops then, once you have wrapped the hands with yarn, embroider stitches onto each hand where thumbs would be. Wrap yarn over the stitches to blend the thumbs into the rest of the hand then cover the arm with evenly wrapped yarn. Ⓐ

With pod hands

Take a pipe-cleaner and cover ½in (12mm) of the end with yarn. Ⓐ Fold over and cover the mound with two or three layers of yarn. Blend the hand into the wrist area with wrapped yarn. Ⓑ Continue wrapping up from the wrist section and cover the arm frame with even layers of yarn. Ⓒ You can make the hands bigger by increasing the length of pipe-cleaner you fold over and by folding over the hand mound a second time before wrapping with more yarn. You can also apply more yarn to broaden the width of the arm.

Will anyone notice I'm wearing Ladybug's slippers?

145

Templates

All templates need to be photocopied at 200% unless otherwise stated

Dragonfly Fairy

Fairy Empress

Buggle Fairy

Florabea Fairy

Fairy Moth

Ladybug Fairy

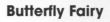

Butterfly Fairy

Grass Sprite

Spooky Hat: Circular brim

Spooky Hat: Cone top

Leaf Blanket
Photocopy at 150%

Spooky Night Cape
Photocopy at 120%

Suppliers

AUSTRALIA

Australian Craft Network Pty Ltd
PO Box 350
Narellan
NSW 2567
Tel: +61 (02) 4648 5053
Fax: +61 (02) 8572 8256
Email: admin@auscraftnet.co.au
www.auscraftnet.com

Threads and More
141 Boundary Road
Bardon
Brisbane 4065
Tel: +61 (07) 3367 0864
Fax: +61 (07) 3367 0458
Email: shop@threadsandmore.co.au
www.threadsandmore.com.au

CANADA

Lewiscraft
www.lewiscraft.ca

Lots of good stuff here

UK

1st For Crafts
South Street
Braintree
Essex
CM7 3HA
Tel: +44 (0) 1376 550099
Fax: +44 (0) 1376 551177
Email: email@1stforcrafts.com
www.1stforcrafts.com

Calico Pie
305 Lancaster Road
Morecambe
Lancs
LA4 5TP
Tel/Fax: +44 (0) 845 1662678
Email: carol@calicopie.co.uk
www.calicopie.co.uk

English Yarns
19 East Street
Shoreham-by-Sea
West Sussex
BN43 5ZE
Tel: +44 (0) 1273 461029
Fax: +44 (0) 1273 465407
Email: sales@englishyarns.co.uk
www.englishyarns.co.uk

Fred Aldous
37 Lever Street
Manchester
M1 1LU
Tel: +44 (0) 8707 517301
Fax: +44 (0) 8707 517303
Email: aldous@btinternet.com
www.fredaldous.co.uk

Hobbicraft
40 Woodhouse Lane
Merrion Centre
Leeds
LS2 8LX
Email: mail@hobbicraft.co.uk
www.hobbicraft.co.uk

Hobbycraft
PO Box 5591
BH23 6YU
Tel: +44 (0) 800 272387
www.hobbycraft.co.uk

Peachey Ethknits
6–7 Edwards Walk
Maldon
Essex
CM9 5PS
Tel: +44 (0) 1621 857102
Email: ethknits@ethknits.co.uk
www.ethknits.co.uk

Stitch1 Knit 1
Tel: +44 (0) 845 6018823
www.stitch1knit1.com

Texere Yarns
College Mill
Barkerend Road
Bradford, West Yorkshire
BD1 4AU
Tel: +44 (0) 1274 722191
Email: info @texere.co.uk
www.texere.co.uk

USA

CraftAmerica.com
498 Dreyfus Road
Berea
KY 40403
Tel: +1 877 306 9178
Email: info@craftamerica.com
www.craftamerica.com

Crafts, etc!
(Domestic) Tel: 1806 888 0321
(International) Tel: +1 405 745 1200
www.craftsetc.com

Walmart
www.walmart.co

Index

See ya!